Cooking With Dysart's

Cooking With Dysart's

stories and recipes from over forty years

Content *Allison Frazier*
Photographs *Mary Hartt*
Design *Allison Frazier*

Printed in Lewiston, Maine at Penmor Printing

Special thanks to Bruce Kennett for his design inspiration and for the laughs.

Thank you to everyone who graciously gave us permission to compile and reprint their content, especially the Bangor Daily News, The Salt Institute for Documentary Studies, and the very talented illustrator Chris VanDusen.

photo locations:

Breakfast
(clockwise from top)
Somes Sound, Cis Stream, Seawall, South Newburgh

Breads and Rolls
(clockwise from top)
Cape Jellison, Cis Stream, Rt. 11 near Brownville, Dixmont, Beech Hill Pond, Machias Seal Island

Soups, Stews, and Chowders
Portland Headlight

Maine Dishes
(clockwise from top)
Eagle Lake Railroad, Mt. Katahdin, Dixmont, Baxter State Park

Fish and Seafood
(clockwise from top)
Southwest Harbor, Stonington, Mount Desert Island, Southwest Harbor

Desserts
(clockwise from top)
Burlington, near Thunder Hole, Dixmont, Echo Lake

Pies
(clockwise from top)
Northern Maine Woods, Cutler, Rt. 11 near Brownville, Sand Beach, Asticou

Cookies and Squares
(clockwise from top)
Caribou, Campobello Island, Grand Falls, Caribou, Ellsworth

contents

When Dave Dysart was planning the first menu, he naturally thought of the best meals he'd ever eaten at Northern Maine logging camps. There, the steady menu consisted of pork and beans three times a day. The cook prepared and the men consumed bushels of cookies, potatoes, pies, breads, and gallons of coffee. Dave knew if he could bring the essence of a woods camp to Bangor, truck drivers would be happy. He searched high and low for the best camp cook until he found Greg Feeney. Now Greg could make pot roast melt in your mouth and the bread better than you have ever tasted.

All through the winter of '67 Dave and Greg planned the way Dysart's would be. Big plates full of food. The menu had to have baked beans everyday. Homemade bread would be served at meal-time, and there would be hot biscuits at lunch. And who wants to be limited to morning when they have a hankering for a good, hearty breakfast?

When Dave was alive, he did his best to keep the original menu. At least once a week he would lecture his daughter Mary, who now manages the restaurant, on slight variations he detected. "Did you let the baker add more cinnamon to the apple pie?" or "This chop suey is too spicy. Greg didn't make it this way." Mary now has free range of the menu, but aside from sneaking in healthier versions of some items, and adding some variety, she has stayed true to the food Dysart's was founded on in 1967.

Like the recipe book we published in 2000, which has raised over $100,000 to date, all proceeds of this project will be donated to Cancer charities in Dave's memory. Within the two covers of this book you will find the recipes that have represented Dysart's for all of these years, but there is much more. We will take you behind the scenes in the restaurant kitchen, let you know why we cook with as many local foods as possible and where they come from. You will even learn a little about trucker terms over the CB radio. You will be treated to many stories, articles, and photos that we hope appeal to the broad array of customers we welcome into our family everyday.

Thank you for visiting, reading, and cooking with us!

Quick Service For Vehicles, Drivers

READY TO GO — Making a last minute check to be sure that everything is ready for this weekend's grand opening of Dysart's Truck Stop on the Coldbrook Road in Hermon are, left to right, Edward Dysart, David Dysart, and Milton Dysart. (NEWS Photo by Hall)

"We emphasize quick service for both the truck and its driver." This is the working motto of the new Dysart Truck Stop on the Coldbrook Road in Hermon.

"Home For The Truckers"

According to Edward R. Dysart, the truck stop is designed around the driver and his needs. The facilities are provided to make the Stop a "home for the truckers."

The Truck Stop, which is run by Dysart, his wife Daisy, their son, David, and his wife, Irene, and his cousin's son, Milton Dysart, offers practically anything a driver could ask for. Naturally there is diesel fuel (four dual pumps of it, in fact), as well as regular gasoline. There is a four- truck garage to keep the trucks running in top condition. But the Dysart Truck Stop aims at keeping the drivers as well as the trucks in top shape for the long hauls.

Variety Of Services

For example, if a trucker is hungry he can have a quick meal at the lunch bar while his truck is being refueled or, if he'd rather, he may enjoy a leisurely supper in the restaurant which is open to the public as well as to truckers. If he'd rather simply relax for a few moments, he may take advan-

JUN 23 1967

Stressed By Dysart Truck Stop

tage of the commodious lounge equipped with television, phonograph, and comfortable chairs. There are rooms for drivers who wish a good night's rest before continuing on the road. There are also showers provided. In addition, there is a store which carries everything from candy to shoes.

Began In 1920

Ed Dysart and his family are well prepared to anticipate the needs of the truckers. Dysart began in the trucking business in 1920 "when everyone bought a truck and started carrying freight." Dysart Transportation grew with the rest of the trucking industry.

Then in 1934 the Dysarts opened their first Truck Stop on Hammond Street where they remained until 1958. Then, as now, their emphasis was on quick service.

"Our relation with the trucking industry in two of its aspects has helped us determine what the drivers need and want," Edward Dysart explained.

In operation for four weeks, Dysart's Truck Stop officially opens this weekend. Taking almost a year to complete, the Truck Stop now employs 24 men and, when operations begin on a full scale, will employ about 30, Dysart explained.

REFUELING STOP — These trucks are being refueled at the new Dysart Truck Stop on the Coldbrook Road in Hermon while their drivers are relaxing in the comfortable lounge or having a bite to eat at the lunch bar. (NEWS Photo by Hall)

breakfast

Dysart's on Facebook

The word "waffle" comes from the french word for honeycomb, which was used to describe the distinctive pattern created by the waffle iron. Originally a much lighter and crispier treat (think of a cannoli), the Belgian variety is generally what we think of as the ultimate breakfast item. Designed to contain deep wells to trap butter and syrup, the waffles are crispy on the outside and smooth and delicious on the inside.

One Facebook fan (join our Facebook community for news, menu updates, and special offers) asked why it is that waffles are only served until 11am. There is no great secret for why- we just simply don't have room in the kitchen to keep the waffle irons running all day. The irons are replaced by stacks of hamburger buns and hotdog rolls that will be needed when the lunch menu starts cranking.

waffles

2 eggs

1 3/4 cups milk

2 cups flour

4 tsp. baking powder

1 tbsp. sugar

1/4 tsp. salt

4 tbsp. melted butter

1 tsp. vanilla extract

Sift dry ingredients into a large bowl. Stir in the melted butter, milk and vanilla. Beat the egg yolks and add them to the dry mixture.

Beat the egg whites with a whisk until they form stiff peaks and carefully fold them into the rest of the ingredients so as not to loose the airy volume.

Using a waffle iron, pour about 1/2 cup of batter onto the griddle and close the lid. Cook for about 3-5 minutes, or until golden.

raspberry sauce

2 cups of fresh or frozen raspberries

2 tbsp. cornstarch

1 cup cold water

1 tsp. lemon juice

1/2 cup sugar

If you are cooking for a large crowd, you can keep them warm in a low temperature oven, but you will lose some of the crispiness. Waffles can also be frozen and come back to life remarkably well in the toaster.

Combine the raspberries, sugar, and lemon juice in a saucepan. Whisk the cornstarch into the cold water until smooth. Add the mixture to the saucepan and bring to a boil.

Simmer for about 5 minutes, stirring constantly, until the desired consistency is reached. The sauce will thicken further as it cools.

Serve warm or cold. The sauce will keep in the refrigerator for up to two weeks.

afro pancakes

Night manager Gail Chaisson was walking past a table when she heard one of her servers tell a customer, "No, they're not bigger than your head, but almost!"

Gail has been in the truckstop environment for enough years to know that a statement like that can get you in trouble around here, so she asked the server what she had been talking about.

The server explained: The young man sitting at her table told her that the last time he was in, the pancakes were bigger than his head and wanted to know if they were still that big. The server told her manager that, "since his present hairstyle was a significantly sized afro", she felt comfortable answering 'No' to his question!

Our pancakes might not have been bigger than this man's head, but they sure do fill up a plate! Not too many orders of Dysart's 'tall stacks' are eaten in their entirety.

pancakes

1 egg

1 1/4 cups flour

1 1/4 cups milk

1/2 tsp. baking soda

1 tsp. sugar

2 tbsp. shortening

1 tsp. baking powder

1/2 tsp. salt

Pre-heat the griddle/frying pan on medium while mixing the batter so the surface is the right temperature right when the batter hits it.

Beat together the egg, milk, and baking soda. Add sugar, shortening, baking powder, salt, and flour. Mix with a whisk until smooth.

Pour batter on the heated grill in round circles. The pancakes can be made thick or thin as desired. Watch the surface of the pancake. When bubbles form and the edges begin to look dry, gently lift one edge of the pancake to check for color. Golden brown means ready to flip.

Blueberry Pancakes
Follow above recipe – and add ½ cup of fresh or frozen Maine blueberries to the batter, folding in carefully at the end.

Blueberry Sauce for topping:

Combine the blueberries, sugar, and lemon juice in a saucepan. Whisk the cornstarch into the cold water until smooth. Add the mixture to the saucepan and bring to a boil. Add cinnamon.

Simmer for about 5 minutes, stirring constantly, until the desired consistency is reached. The sauce will thicken further as it cools.

Serve warm or cold. The sauce will keep in the refrigerator for up to two weeks.

blueberry sauce:

4 1/2 cups blueberries

1 cup water

3/4 tsp. lemon juice

1/2 cup sugar

2 tbsp. corn starch

1/2 tsp. cinnamon

cooking with flashlights

The Ice Storm of 1998 lasted almost 3 weeks and left over half of Maine's population without power for much of that time. All 16 Maine counties were declared federal disaster areas, and FEMA-eligible costs totaled $48 million. Disaster had struck all of the homes in the area leaving many cold and hungry. Dysart's, certainly not untouched by the damages, tried to do their best to continue business despite limited resources.

Running on a small generator (which was immediately upgraded after the storm settled) the restaurant was heated and an abridged menu was created. The industrial coffee makers required too much power to run, so a stepladder was stationed near the machines and it was one man's job to very slowly pour hot water through the grinds. The wait staff, generally some of the restaurant's biggest coffee consumers, shared mugs to reduce the number of dishes that needed to be hand washed. And pocket-sized flashlights were shared amongst customers who needed to make a trip to the restroom.

pumpkin pancakes

2 cups all-purpose flour

3 tbsp. brown sugar

1 tbsp. baking powder

1 tsp. baking soda

1 tbsp. pumpkin pie spice

1/2 tsp. salt

1 1/2 cups milk

1 cup pumpkin puree

1 egg

2 tbsp. vegetable oil

1 cup chocolate chips (optional)

Without the ability to run the whole kitchen, the breakfast menu was reduced to just pancakes. Mary Hartt, restaurant manager, had one particular customer very upset that she couldn't order an omelet. Mary apologized and explained, "I am sorry, but we are cooking with flashlights on a very small cooking surface so all we can offer this morning are pancakes."

The lady was very rude when she continued to complain that the only reason she came here was for an omelette and she didn't understand what the problem was. Mary very politely suggested that she go home and make herself an omelette. The woman turned red and raised her voice to tell her, "I can't make an omelette, I don't have any power!" Mary calmly replied, "So would you like plain or blueberry?"

Mix together the milk, pumpkin, egg, and oil. Combine the flour, brown sugar, baking powder, baking soda, pumpkin pie spice, and salt. Stir into the pumpkin mixture just enough to combine.

Heat a lightly oiled griddle or frying pan over medium high heat. Pour or scoop the batter onto the griddle, using approximately 1/4 cup for each pancake. Lightly sprinkle chocolate chips onto the tops of the pancakes before flipping (optional). Brown on both sides and serve.

there's only one condition

Lynne Noyes, a longtime waitress here, has an interesting bartering tradition with some family out of town. This trade off began years ago when her in-laws came up from the coast to Bangor to visit for the weekend.

"Of course, no trip to Bangor would be complete without a breakfast visit to Dysart's. Okay, maybe it was even a 2 AM visit. None the less, they asked me for my suggestion, and my first recommendation for breakfast is always Dave's Hash. Well, they loved it. We even had to make a second stop back to the restaurant before they left to go back to the coast. For the record, this time it was during the real breakfast hour. Low and behold, this time it tasted as good at 9:00 AM as it did at 2:00 AM."

Being the good family participants that they are, one great family visit deserves another, so Lynne and Frank agreed to go to the coast for their turn the following weekend.

When Thursday night rolled around, they got a phone call telling them that they know lots of the lobstermen in the area, and they would have a feast of lobsters and steamers for them when they got there.

"Oh wait, this is on one condition. Can you bring some of Dave's Hash?"

And so the tradition began...

The secret is making sure that you chop your meat and dice your potatoes into the same size pieces. In the restaurant we use a grinder with large holes.

Combine equal quantities of chopped, cooked corned beef and diced potatoes. Add the chopped onion. Season with salt and pepper. Shape into patties of about 5 ounces.

Heat butter in a large skillet (preferably cast iron) on medium heat. Place patties in the skillet and let them brown. If you hear them sizzling, this is good.

Press down again with the spatula. If there is too much sticking, you can add a little more butter to the pan. Continue to cook in this manner until the potatoes and the corned beef are nicely browned.

Dave's hash

4 cups cooked Maine potatoes, peeled and cut into ½ inch cubes

4 cups cooked corned beef

1 large onion, diced

2 tbsp. butter

1 tsp. salt

1 tsp. pepper

Mix flour, sugar, salt, and baking powder together in a bowl. Lightly beat the eggs and then add eggs, oil, vanilla, and milk to dry ingredients. Mix together until moistened. Now you can add the additional ingredients [suggested variations to the right] to make the muffins you desire.

Sprinkle cinnamon and sugar on top of muffins (optional).

Preheat oven to 400 degrees. When you put the muffins in the heated oven, turn the temperature down to 350. Bake for 15 minutes turn in oven bake for another 15 minutes. Check with a toothpick to make sure the muffins are done. Pick should come out of muffin clean.

basic muffin recipe

4 cups all purpose flour

1 cup sugar

1 tsp. salt

2 tbsp. baking powder

2 eggs

1/2 cup oil

1 tbsp. vanilla

2 to 2 ¼ cups milk

To make the following muffin variations, add the additional ingredients listed to the basic recipe (unless otherwise stated). Follow the standard baking directions. While we always prefer to use fresh berries when they are available, frozen berries can be thawed and drained of excess water before adding to the mix.
Adding a cup of finely chopped walnuts is an option to almost any muffin.

Baking Tips:

Pans should be greased very well. This will prevent the dough from sticking to the sides and rise better.

Using an ice cream scoop will help to ensure all the tins are filled the same. This will make the muffins more uniform in size.

You should take the muffins out of the tins immediately after they are done. This will prevent them from steaming and getting soggy.

Internal temperature of muffins should be above 200 degrees when fully cooked.

At high altitudes, reduce baking powder by ¼ tsp.

Blueberry: Add 4 cups of blueberries.

Raspberry: Add 4 cups of raspberries.

Bumbleberry: Add 2 cups blueberries and 2 cups raspberries.

Very Berry: Add a combination of blueberries, raspberries, and blackberries totalling 4 cups.

Apple Nut: Add 3 cups apples, 1 cup finely chopped walnuts, and 1 tsp. cinnamon.

Orange Cranberry: Add (2) 11oz. cans of mandarin oranges (drained and cut into small pieces), 1 cup dried cranberries, and 2 tsp. orange extract.

Hawaiian: Add (1)15oz. can pineapple (drained and cut into small pieces), 1 cup of shredded coconut, 1 cup of maraschino cherries cut into small pieces, and 2 tsp. coconut extract.

Peanut Butter Banana: Add 5 or 6 ripe bananas, mashed, and 1 cup peanut butter, plain or crunchy.

Peach Raspberry: Add 2 cups of raspberries, and 2 cups of canned peaches (drained)

Strawberry Rhubarb: Add 2 cups of rhubarb and 2 cups of strawberries.

Chocolate Chip: Decrease sugar in recipe to 1/2 cup. Add about 2 cups of semi-sweet chocolate chips.

Chocolate Chocolate Chip: Add ¾ cup baking cocoa to the chocolate chip muffins.

Cinnamon Chip: Decrease sugar in recipe by half, add 2 cups cinnamon chips.

Apple Cinnamon: Add 3 cups chopped apples and 1 cup cinnamon chips. If you can't find cinnamon chips you can add 1 to 2 tsp. of ground cinnamon.

secret recipe

Mary Dysart Hartt, who, like her two brothers, has been in the restaurant since she was very young, has always loved horses. When she was younger her father used to take her to a horse show every winter in Scottsdale, Arizona to see the Arabian horses she loved so much.

A vendor at the event was selling cinnamon buns, so Mary asked her father to have one the first day for breakfast. These were not your ordinary sticky buns. Day after day as the word spread, the line for these treats got longer and longer. In true businessman spirit, Dave was determined to get this recipe and bring it back to make for his restaurant.

"It took me three years to convince the guy to give me the recipe. Finally, I persuaded him that we were too far away to give him any competition." Dave promised he would never give away the recipe, and for years he would vaguely answer, "the big secret is lots of butter."

Making these cinnamon buns for a large crowd is quite the production, which is why the restaurant only offers them on weekends and when they are gone, they are gone. Dave promised he would never reveal the secret recipe, but that doesn't mean that we can't! These are surely something your family will love.

cinnamon buns

1 batch of white bread dough

1 cup softened butter

1 cup sugar

1/4 cup cinnamon

Cinnamon Bun Sauce

1/2 cup butter

3/4 cup light karo syrup

1 1/2 cups brown sugar

Make a batch of the white bread dough according to directions (pg 30) and after the second rising, roll it out into a rectangle until the dough is about 1/2" thick.
Spread with softened butter, and sprinkle the cinnamon sugar mixture on top. Roll up tightly, starting with the wide side of the rectangle. Seal the roll well by pinching the dough on the edges.

Cut roll into 1" slices, and place them evenly spaced to allow for spreading on a greased baking sheet. Cover and let rise again for 30 minutes. Bake at 375°F for 25-30 minutes until golden brown and completely baked through. Makes about 2 dozen 5" rolls.

Melt butter in a medium saucepan. Add brown sugar to melted butter and stir well until the mixture is smooth. Let simmer for ½ hour.
Add karo syrup to butter mixture and simmer for another ½ hour.
Pour over cinnamon buns and serve.

Aunt Kate gets frugal

Aunt Kate was 77 when the current Dysart's location opened, and when she passed away years later, she had dozens of doughnut loving great-great grandchildren. For years Kate made her delicious doughnuts by hand, using a recipe that she had been famous for.

The family knew that Kate's doughnuts would be a big hit at the truckstop, so they began purchasing them from her to serve with hot coffee. As the years went by, Kate grew more frugal, and in turn, the size of the doughnuts shrunk significantly. Choosing not to make any waves with dear Aunt Kate, the restaurant started serving two of her now-mini doughnuts instead of one.

We hope you enjoy making these as much as you will enjoy eating them!

Aunt Kate's molasses doughnuts

2 eggs

1 cup molasses

1 cup buttermilk or sour milk

4 1/2 to 5 1/2 cups of flour

1 1/2 tsp. baking soda

1/2 tsp. ginger

1 tsp. cinnamon

1 tsp. vanilla

3 tbsp. melted shortening

1/2 tsp. salt

Fry in deep fat at 370 to 380 degrees.

Beat eggs in bowl first, then add molasses and buttermilk. Add the rest of the ingredients, and enough flour to make a soft dough easy to roll.

Chill dough for easier handling. Roll doughnuts out onto lightly-floured board and cut with a doughnut cutter. Fry on one side until doughnut splits a little on the top (about 3 min) and then turn over and fry on the other side until done.

Drain on absorbent paper. To sugar the doughnuts, shake doughnuts one at a time in a small paper bag with granulated sugar while still warm enough for the sugar to stick.

When Kate made these doughnuts she fried them in lard.

third generation

Ed Dysart, President of Dysart's, is the third generation of his family to run this long-standing family business. He sits in the front office where his father did, and is known for staying true to the philosophy that Dysart's was established on.

Excerpt from The Greater Bangor Business Monthly
October 1995

"Imagine the 40 acres (plus or minus a couple of acres) of land that sits adjacent to the Interstate 95 Coldbrook Road exit as a vacant lot.

Ed Dysart doesn't have to imagine. He just reaches into his memory bank and he can pull out the mental pictures of what the landscape was like before and during the construction and evolution of Dysart's- truckstop, gas station, restaurant, and home-away-from-home for truckers.

Ed, now 43, was a junior in high school when construction started on what was at the time the new, improved version of the family's business. "I remember helping on the site work here. I was a junior in high school and I didn't have my driver's license yet, but I'd be out here driving a dump truck hauling the dirt around," he said during a recent interview in his office.

In the 1930's, Edward Dysart, the grandfather whom today's general manager was named after, believed to survive and prosper, you needed to be "customer oriented and have a good quality product at a reasonable price. That's what we're trying to do today," the founder's grandson said."

sausage gravy over biscuits

8 warm biscuits
(page 42)

1 lb. ground pork

4 cups milk

1 tsp. poultry seasoning

1/4 tsp. thyme

salt and pepper to taste

roux

1/4 cup butter

1/4 cup flour

Short cut to sausage and gravy - keep a roux (butter paste) in a jar in refrigerator. Roux is made with equal amounts of melted butter and flour blended together.

Brown the ground pork in a skillet. Don't drain, traditionally it is left with it's own fat. Set aside for later.

Heat the milk to a boil over low heat. Whisk in the roux. Add seasonings. Stir constantly until mixture boils for 1 min. Stir in cooked ground pork. Remove from heat. If the sauce is too thick, stir in more milk.

breads and rolls

tap it out

Most professional bakers have a keen sense for tapping the bottom of a pan and checking for a hollow sound to test for bread to be done. If you're new to this technique, try doing this every five minutes toward the end of baking and you'll hear how the sound changes. If you don't know what you are listening for, use a thermometer to test the internal temperature. All breads are done around 195°.

Use ½ cup of the warm water and mix with sugar and yeast in a large bowl or the bowl of a mixer. Let it set for 10 minutes to proof. The yeast will bubble.

Add the remaining water, milk, salt, and oil.

Begin adding the flour, a cup at a time, mixing with a wooden spoon or dough hook if using a mixer. Mix until the dough is fairly firm and only slightly sticky. The dough will come together and begin to leave the sides of the bowl.

Turn the dough out onto a lightly floured board to knead. Kneading is done by folding the dough over towards you and pressing with the heel of your hand.

Add more flour to make the dough smooth and elastic (this can be done with the mixer with a hook). Place dough in a warm place and let rise in an oiled bowl until doubled in bulk.

white bread

(4 loaves)

2 1/2 cups warm water (100° F)

2 cups warm milk (100° F)

2 packages yeast, active dry

4 tbsp. sugar

2 tsp. salt

1/4 cup vegetable oil

flour to make stiff dough (10 cups)

Grease 4 (4x8) bread pans with oil. Punch the dough down, turn out onto a lightly floured board and divide into 4 equal portions. Shape into 4 loaves and place, seam side down in the prepared pans to rise again in a warm place.

Bake at 350°F for 40 to 45 minutes. There is a tapping method where a tap can tell you the bread is done. If you are unsure of your tapping ability use a thermometer. At 195°F to 200°F the bread is done.

To make rolls:

Follow the recipe for white bread. After they have risen punch the dough down and turn out onto a lightly floured board. We divide the dough into 2 oz. portions and roll into a ball. The experienced bakers can roll with both hands filling a 18 by 12 pan with 2 ½ dozen rolls in just over a minute.
Home bakers can shape the dough as desired and bake until golden on top.

proof positive

Rising dough is sensitive to drafts, so make sure to keep the dough covered and away from cold areas during rise time. In the restaurant we delay the dough by placing it in the walk-in (refrigerator) to bake later, so if you have room you can do this and bake your bread or rolls just before you want to serve them.

Have you ever had our mouth-watering rolls hot out of the oven at five? They were rolled sometime in the morning and delayed by the cold, but baked just in time for you to enjoy with your dinner.

Use ½ cup of the warm water taken from the total amount. Mix with sugar and yeast in a large bowl or the bowl of a mixer. This needs to proof for 10 minutes. The yeast will bubble.

Add the remaining water, milk, salt and oil. Mix well.

Begin adding the wheat flour, one cup at a time, mixing with a wooden spoon or dough hook if using a mixer. Then add white flour, a cup at a time and mix until dough is fairly firm and only slightly sticky. The dough will begin to leave the sides of the bowl.

Turn the dough out onto a lightly floured board to knead. Kneading is done by folding the dough over towards you and pressing away from you with the heel of your hand. Add more flour to make the dough smooth and elastic. (This can be done with the mixer with a hook) Place dough in a warm place and let rise in an oiled bowl until doubled in bulk. At Dysart's we use a proofer, a box designed to maintain 100 degrees. An oven can be used to proof with a pan of hot water on another shelf to keep the dough from drying out.

Grease 4 bread pans with oil. Punch the dough down, turn out onto a lightly floured board and divide into 4 equal portions. Shape into 4 loaves and place, seam side down in the prepared pans to rise again in a warm place.

Bake at 350 for 40 to 45 minutes. Try out your 'tapping' skills (previous page) but if you are unsure, use a thermometer. At 195 F. to 200 F. the bread is done.

wheat bread
(4 loaves)

2 1/2 cups warm water (100 F)

2 cups warm milk (100 F)

2 packages yeast, active dry

4 tbsp. sugar

¼ cup vegetable oil

4 cups wheat flour

6 cups white flour

water it

When you are making bread, water is a very important ingredient because it is needed to dissolve the yeast and helps activate it. Even when a recipe lists milk, you will find it will call for at least ¼ cup of water per package of yeast. Oil adds flavor and make breads tender and moist, while eggs add color, and richness. Lastly, your sugar will give your loaf a nice golden crust and sweeten the dough.

The amount of flour needed in a recipe may vary according to the type of flour, how old it is, and it's moisture content. Try to stay within the amount called for in a recipe but don't worry if you need a little less or a little more.

molasses oatmeal bread
(4 loaves)

2 1/2 cups warm water (100 F)

2 cups warm milk (100 F)

2 packages yeast, active dry

1/2 cup molasses

2 eggs

2 tsp. salt

1/4 cup vegetable oil

2 cups oatmeal

flour to make stiff dough (8 cups)

2 tbsp. sugar

1 extra cup of oatmeal for the crust

Use ½ cup of the warm water and mix with sugar and yeast in a large bowl or the bowl of a mixer. Let it set, as this needs to proof for 10 minutes. The yeast will bubble.

Add the remaining water, milk, salt, eggs, molasses, oatmeal, and oil. Mix well.

Begin adding the flour, a cup at a time, mixing with a wooden spoon or dough hook if using a mixer. Mix until the dough is fairly firm and only slightly sticky. The dough will begin to leave the sides of the bowl.

Turn the dough out onto a lightly floured board to knead. Kneading is done by folding the dough over towards you and pressing with the heel of your hand.

Add more flour to make the dough smooth and elastic. (This can be done with the mixer with a hook) Place dough in a warm place and let rise in an oiled bowl until doubled in bulk. (At Dysart's we use a proofer which is a box designed to hold the bread 100 F.) You can place it in an oven with a pan of water to make sure the dough doesn't dry out too much.

Grease 4 (4x8) bread pans with oil. Punch the dough down, turn out onto a lightly floured board and divide into 4 equal portions. Shape into 4 loaves and roll the tops in oatmeal for a nice outside crust. Place the formed dough, seam side down in the prepared pans to rise again a warm place for 20 minutes.

Bake at 350 F. for 40 to 45 minutes. There is a tapping method where a tap can tell you the bread is done. If you are unsure of your tapping ability use a thermometer. At 195 F to 200 F the bread is done.

In 1957, Dysart's was a 50's truckstop selling fuel and making truck repairs. Originally located on Hammond Street in Bangor, the location was displaced along with 2 family homes, to accommodate the bridge over Insterstate 95.

raisin bread

2 packages yeast, active dry

2 cups of milk scalded and cooled

1/2 cup of butter or shortening

1 tsp. salt

3/4 cup sugar

3 eggs

1/2 to 1 tsp. cinnamon, to taste

1 1/2 cups raisins

8 cups flour (you may need less or more depending on the weather or other factors beyond your control)

In a small bowl soak your yeast in ½ cup of warm water. Scald milk and cool to about 90 degrees. (see below for scalding instructions)

Cream together butter, salt, and sugar. Add beaten eggs, cinnamon, raisins, yeast, and cooled milk . Work in enough flour to make a soft dough. Set dough in a bowl and cover so it doesn't dry out. Let rise until it doubles in size.

Shape dough into bread loaf. Place into a bread pan and bake at 350 degrees for about 1 hour. Turn half way through. The inside temperature when done should be 195 to 200 degrees.

Scalding milk: Bring it nearly to a boil (185°F), preferably in a thick-bottomed pan, and stirring actively, to keep a protein skin from forming on the surface and to keep the proteins and sugar from sticking to the bottom of the pan. If you don't scald your milk before using it, there is a chance that the volume of your bread will be affected and it may not rise as much as you would like.

super frog

Normand R. Lajoie was just being served his lunch special when I sat down at the trucker's table to have a chat with him. His rosy face and crisp salmon dress shirt helped him stand out amongst the sea of navy and grey, but did nothing compared to the attention he was getting from the Dysart's staff that day.

"When you come here with a legend, you get better service," joked Lajoie's friend who joined us a few minutes later, "All the girls come over and give him a kiss on the cheek. I am hoping for a little peck one of these days."

Everyone here knows Lajoie as "Super Frog", who got his name from the illuminated frog that perched on the top of his tractor-trailer for as long as anyone can remember. He was here when Dave Dysart cleared the bushes to make room for the fuel area, and can recall and re-tell hundreds of stories since then.

Lajoie hails from Cyr Plantation, (near Van Buren) where he took over his family's potato farm at the age of 17. He began hauling the spuds all around the state shortly after. 56 years later, and only a day before we met for lunch, Lajoie proudly received the award of "Farm Family of the Year" from the Maine Potato Board.

He shared many of the stories you will read about on other pages, along with excessively detailed stories of each of his 8 children and 28 grandchildren. Just when I felt that I had enough information to crash any family wedding, he called me back. "Oh jeeze" he said, "Don't forget to mention my wife Maxine. We've been married 52 years and she has been the backbone behind it all."

banana bread

1 1/2 cups all purpose flour

1 tsp. baking soda

1/2 tsp. salt

1/4 cup butter or margarine

1 cup sugar

1 egg

3 ripe, mashed bananas

1/2 cup finely chopped walnuts (optional)

Cream together sugar, butter, and eggs until fluffy.

Mash bananas with a fork until they are softened, but not too liquid. Add bananas to mixture and beat one at a time.

Fold in remaining ingredients and mix until moistened.

Pour into a greased 5 x 9 inch loaf pan. Bake approximately 60 minutes at 350 degrees. Be careful not to overcook or bread will be dry. Loosen the sides of the loaf from the pan, and let cool for at least 30 minutes before slicing.

"The atmosphere is a mixed bag. It all depends on the time of day. Usually, there's an eclectic mix of diners. You'll find late model Mercedes Benz owners dining next to people who own cars where you have a hard time telling where the Bondo ends and the car begins.

And, usually, there is an assortment of today's American Cowboy: the trucker. Late nights, or early mornings, depending on your point of view, you also find a few people who have had more than their share of adult beverages.

Dysart's remains a popular place to eat after last call at the Bangor-area nightspots."

The Greater Bangor Business Monthly, October 1995

pumpkin nut bread

2 1/2 cups all purpose flour

2 eggs

1 1/2 cups sugar

1/2 tsp. baking soda

2 tsp. baking powder

1 tsp. cinnamon

1/4 tsp. nutmeg

1/4 tsp. ground cloves

1/2 cup vegetable oil

1 (16oz.) can pumpkin puree

1 cup raisins or chocolate chips

1 cup walnuts (optional)

In a bowl combine sugar, oil, and eggs; beat until fluffy. Mix in pumpkin well with a whisk or on low if using a mixer.

In a small bowl combine all dry ingredients and mix together make sure there are no lumps and everything is well combined.

Add dry ingredients to pumpkin mixture until all moistened. Do not over mix.

Pour into a greased 5 x 9 inch loaf pan. Bake at 350 degrees for 55 to 60 minutes. Check with toothpick to see if done. Pick should come out clean.

Variation:
Instead of raisins you can add chocolate chips to make the most wonderful pumpkin chocolate chip bread. You can also choose to make this batter into muffins- just decrease the cooking time and make sure the tins are well greased.

biscuits with every meal

biscuits

2 cups of all-purpose flour

1 tbsp. baking powder

1/2 tsp. baking soda

1/2 tsp. salt

1 tbsp. sugar

1/3 cup shortening

3/4 cup milk

cinnamon sugar biscuits:

above biscuit ingredients

1 cup sugar

1 tbsp. cinnamon

1/2 cup of melted butter

whole wheat biscuits:
substitute ½ cup whole wheat for ½ cup of the white flour.

In 1967, when Dysart's opened and Betty Feeney was the pastry cook, she would make cinnamon sugar biscuits for lunch everyday. Once the dough was rolled out, she could be seen cutting the round biscuits out of the dough batch with machine like precision and speed. The flaky dough was then dipped into butter and rolled in cinnamon and sugar making a sweet crust that was hard to beat.

Today in the restaurant, biscuits are one of the items that are served throughout the day. You can always get a grilled biscuit as your bread choice with your eggs and bacon at breakfast time. Biscuits are a big seller with soups, stews, and especially fish chowder. And our strawberry shortcake just wouldn't be the same without the warm, fresh baked biscuits to absorb all of the delicious strawberry juices.

Preheat oven to 450 F. Mix the flour, baking powder, baking soda, sugar, and salt. Cut in the shortening until you have coarse crumbs. Mixture should be like a meal.

Add almost all the milk all at once and mix very gently until flour is moistened. Use enough to make a soft, puffy dough easy to roll out. Too much milk makes the dough sticky. Not enough makes biscuits dry.

Turn out dough out on a lightly-floured board (trying not to handle too much) Roll out to an even ½ inch thickness. Using a 2 inch cutter or a glass. Place biscuits close together for soft sides, an inch apart for crusty sides. Bake until golden brown or inside temperature is 195 F

Cinnamon Sugar Biscuits
1 cup cinnamon sugar (1 tablespoon cinnamon mixed in 1 cup of sugar)
½ cup of butter.

To make cinnamon sugar biscuits: Follow the above recipe except after the biscuits are cut out dip them in the butter and then roll in the cinnamon sugar.

As the old saying goes, the only thing that stays the same is that everything changes. There have been a number of changes to the business and the restaurant over the years, but for the most part, Dysart's has been able to maintain a consistent image and foothold in the community. The Dysart family just loves this gem of an article written in 1986, and can't help but chuckle at just how well the feeling of the Trucker's Room was captured by words alone.

Around the Clock at Dysart's

Salt Magazine, number 28, October 1986

Written by Traci Timlin
Photographs taken by Ken Kobre

"**G**oing in to eat?" that man in grey coveralls and cap asks as he holds open the door of Dysart's Truckstop Restaurant. "Here's 87 cents off your meal." He smiles as he hands his fuel credit coupon to a perfect stranger.

"Have a good day now." He nods and hurries outside, weaving his way through the gridlock of revving engines that clog the parking lot. His is just one of the thousand or so trucks that wheel into the truckstop daily off exit 44, just south of Bangor, Maine.

It is morning and the breakfast rush is on. A feeling of early morning laziness envelops the place, despite the chatter of many conversations, the clatter of dishes from the kitchen, the bustle of the waitresses and the traffic in and out the door.

Men come and go constantly, usually alone, sometimes in pairs. There is an air of camaraderie at the long tables running the length of the room. A

cardboard sign hangs from the edge of one red and white checkered tablecloth. "TRUCKERS ONLY."

Thick white coffee mugs, turned bottom up, mark place settings among the organized clutter of condiments: ketchup, sugar, cream, butter, jam, salt, pepper, water pitchers, and thermal coffee pots.

A man in a Dysart's cap sits down and fills his coffee mug. Almost immediately, there is a waitress at his side.

"Morning, Mike. How are you today?"

"Oh, not bad. How 'bout yourself?"

"Same as always, What'll it be this

morning?" She scribbles his order and rushes off to fill a coffee pot that has run dry at the far end of the table, picking up empty plates and dropping a check with a smile as she passes.

Behind the truckers' tables, a thick brick wall with a now un-used fireplace acts as a barrier between the trucker's dining area and a room for the general public.

Walking into the second dining room is like walking into another world. The checkered tablecloths have given way to the natural wood of the table and small paper placemats, the thick coffee mugs to cups and saucers. Gone are the thermal coffee pots and water pitchers. The tables are grouped in sets of two, four, and six.

It's quieter on this side of the brick wall. People talk softly among themselves or read newspapers. No one calls greetings across the room. The country and western music from the transistor radio on the trucker's side doesn't carry this far. Noise from the kitchen is muffled.

Outside the truckstop, the air is filled with the dull rumbling of engines, the hiss and groan of shifting gears as one trailer slides away from the service island and another one pulls in to take its place.

A truck grinds to a stop alongside a gas pump and it's driver jumps to the ground. He nods hello to the station attendant who carries over a stepladder and climbs up to wash the windshield. The driver stands nearby, stretching, watching for a moment. Convinced that his truck is in good hands, he goes inside to make a phone call, passing a group of truckers in the doorway.

They stand, hands in pockets, talking.

"Like I said, I woulda been gone this morning," says Joseph Morrow, whose friends call him by his middle name, Simon. "But this guy, he needed a hand, so I helped him out. Yeah, I'll be headed outa here pretty quick now."

"Oh sure he will," the man next to him kids. "That's what he said three hours ago, and he's been here two days!" The men laugh good-naturedly. They make no sign of leaving.

"Yeah. I'm going real soon," Simon repeats, rocking back on his heels. He's been coming to Dysart's for about 16 years now, almost as long as Dysart's has been here.

Through the doorway to the left is the supply store. The rows of shelves hold everything from Yosemite Sam mudflaps and billy clubs to antacid and toothpaste.

A young man in a blue work-shirt walks through the circle of men in the doorway into the sunlight. He has just bought five bottles of apple juice. Juggling them with one hand, he digs keys out of his front pocket.

He saunters to his cab, opens the door, and tosses the juice into a cooler on the passenger seat. He walks to the front of the truck. One foot on the bumper, he pulls at the grill and the enormous hood falls forward, exposing the engine. He checks the oil. Wiping his hands on his jeans, he makes a quick circle around the trailer, kicking tires as he goes.

Satisfied that everything is all set, he puts both hands on the hood and with a big heave of this entire body, sends it springing back in place with a dull clank.

Upstairs in the lounge it's quiet. Jimmy Rakes is reading the newspaper. A trucker from North Carolina, he doesn't get up to Bangor very often. Two other occupants of the room relax in worn vinyl chairs that flank either side of the sofa and face the television.

The three truckers are waiting. Waiting to be loaded, unloaded of for their dispatcher to match them up with a haul. "Lifestyles of the Rich and Famous" works its way through the static on the t.v. screen and tries to capture the attention of the truckers.

"So, where ya headed?" Jimmy asks the Texan in the recliner.

"Oh, south." He chuckles. "Ain't nothin' but south from here."

"Got a load yet?" Jimmy's been waiting since yesterday.

"Nope. And if I don't get one by supper, I'm going to head down and find myself one."

"Ain't much of anything up here. I was supposed to pick up a load here this morning. No one seems to know where it's gone to though. Yep. People think you ain't got nothing better to do than wait. I didn't come all the way up here for the view."

"Hey, did you want to come up through Vermont? Now there's a nice drive, the mountains and all…"

"Whaddaya mean 'nice'? You talking about good scenery, or just plain hard work?" The men chuckle to themselves about pulling a fully loaded trailer through the mountains.

"Yeah. Those mountains are something else. I tell ya though," the Texan stops in mid sentence to take a long drag on his cigarette.

"You get down to the Florida coast, now there's a good drive. He flicks his cigarette and leans forward, vinyl creaking as he moves. He sits poised, elbows on knees, hands outstretched.

"I was heading down there in the Keys once. Had some spare time. Thought I'd give it a look and head down. Thought I was nearly there and then I saw this sign for the Keys. Seventy miles it says. I couldn't believe it. You can drive forever out there. Real Scenic."

"You know," Jimmy says. "That's the thing about trucking. People think it's glamorous. They think you get to see a lot. But you don't get to see that much. You're sitting around loading, unloading, getting a load. You don't get to take the time to dump your trailer and drive around and see the sights."

"I hear ya, You're right ya know. Once when I was in Dallas…" The Texan takes over as the conversation drifts from Coastal California to the Boston Harbor, each man sharing his version of the best and most scenic drives in the country.

Somewhere along the road, the static has eaten away at the television screen leaving nothing but white noise. No one seems to notice. The truckers find their own stories far more compelling than the "Lifestyles of the Rich and Famous."

"Once I got this call to deliver a meat shipment," the Texan breaks into a fresh story."

"It was Tuesday morning and they told me it had to be in Boston by the next day. Can you believe it? So I ask this guy, 'Does it really have to be there tomorrow morning?' and he says yes it does.

"Well I thought about it. The price was good and I didn't have a load right then. You have to make a buck when you can. So I said I'd do it.

"Now I've been on these wild goose chases before with guys that think everything has to be there yesterday. And I knew I was going to check it out myself beforehand. Last time I busted my butt to get a load on time, I delivered a load of pipe to this construction site.

"When I pull in early Friday morning, these guys just look at me and say, 'What are you doing here? We didn't expect you 'til Tuesday!' I say, 'I got this load here they tell me had to be here this morning.' They still just look at me.

"Finally one guy says, 'Let me show you something.' So I follow him around this building and they've got pipe stacked as high as the building.

" 'We ain't even used all this yet,' he tells me. 'The crane ain't due 'til Monday morning. I can't unload you 'til then.'

"So there I am, stuck for the weekend. I tell ya that's the last time I've ever hurried to deliver something without checking with the receiver first." Leaning back to flick ash from his cigarette, the Texan pauses, gathering his thoughts before continuing his story.

"So anyway, I pick up the meat shipment and head out for Boston. A ways down the road I give the receiver a call to see what's what. I get this guy, a Mr. Johnson or something.

"And I ask him if I get there tomorrow, will he unload me? He tells me if I can get there before noon he'll do it.

"I say, 'look, I'm in Indiana. You seen a map lately? Do you know how far it is from here to Boston? And you want me there by noon?'

"He just tells me, 'If you're here by twelve, ill unload you. If it's 12:05, you wait till Thursday." So I figure it's worth it and start out as fast as I can.

"Well, I pull into Boston about ten thirty the next morning and the loading dock is empty so I pull right in. This guy comes over and he says to me, 'What are you doing? You can't park here.'

"And I say, 'Oh yes I can. I delivered this shipment and they told me they'd

'Where's this Mr. Johnson?' She says, 'He's probably upstairs in his office.' So I start walking up these stairs and she's yelling after me, 'Hey, you can't go up there!'

"And I just keep walking. It was kinda funny. Here's me, I look terrible, haven't

four feet tall and carrying a clipboard is standing there. 'You Mr. Johnson?' I ask.

"He says yes and I say, 'Look, you promised me if I was here before noon you'd unload me. By my watch it's quarter of eleven. So as I see it, you got to unload me.

"I've been driving all night and I'm tired. I'm going to sleep now. When I wake up, I better be unloaded or I'm gonna take all that meat and stack it outside by the dock there and leave it. Whether you unload me or not, I am pulling out of here as soon as I wake up. I'm not waiting around 'til tomorrow.'

"So I lay back down and go to sleep. A little while later there's another knock on my door and I peek my head out again and say, 'Yeah?'

"This guy says, 'That'll be $150 to unload you,' and I say 'Okay,' and he just stands there. And I say, 'Look, I don't know who's gonna pay your $150, but it ain't gonna be me. All I know is I'm going back to sleep and when I wake up I better be unloaded or all this meat's gonna get stacked up right over there. You're not gonna use my truck and my gas for storage.'

unload me, so unload me.' And this guy says, 'You'll have to come back tomorrow.'

"Now I'm getting fed up with this so I go inside and I say. 'What's the problem? They tell me out there that they can't unload me. I talked to this Mr. Johnson on the phone and he says they can.'

"This lady at the front desk says she can't do anything for me, so I say,

had any sleep and I'm walking around these guys in suits looking for Mr. Johnson.

"He's not in, so I say, 'You tell Mr. Johnson that I'm here. I'll be in my truck sleeping.'

"So I go out to my truck. I leave both doors open so there's a nice breeze and go to sleep. Pretty soon there's a knock on my door and this little guy about

"So I lay back down and go back to sleep. I musta slept, oh about ten hours or so, 'cause when I woke up, it was dark. I sit up and climb into the front seat and I think, 'I wonder if I'm unloaded?'

"I get out of my truck and it's pitch dark. No one's around. Everyone's gone home. So I go around to the back of the truck and sure enough, I'm unloaded. Still don't know who paid that $150."

He leans back into his chair, laughing to himself.

"Yep. That'll teach 'em to rush an order. Any time you get one of those rush orders you tell 'em that you want triple what they want to pay you. Then you find out how soon it really has to be there!"

"The doors have never been locked inthe 18 years we've been open," says Ed Dysart of the truckstop that is his family business.

"We don't even have a key to the doors." Ed leans back in his chair. His office windows face the service island in the parking lot.

"We're never closed," he repeats. "Other than our restaurant that closes down for 24 hours at Christmas time. The pumps out here are still open and we have sandwiches and coffee for anyone travelling through.

"It's a typical family business. I'm the third generation. My grandfather had a freight business in the forties and fifties."

The business was in downtown Bangor. When the Maine turnpike was built, Ed's father, Dave Dysart, moved the truckstop to their present location off Interstate 95. A prime location for a truckstop.

"I'd say half our business is local and also people travelling. It's handy. You don't have to go into the city. It's right off the Interstate. You develop a reputation and it draws people.

"From Canada to Kittery, it's the only one."

Dinner hour has arrived. The tables in the restaurant are nearly all filled. A man in a blue t-shirt stands in the kitchen doorway.

"Not too much ice." He cups his had and calls after a waitress who disappears into the depth of the kitchen.

On the wall next to the kitchen doorway hangs a large red sign. White plastic letters advertise the day's specials along with a long list of homemade desserts: strawberry shortcake, blueberry pie, pineapple upsidedown cake, jello.

Dennis Dugan sits at the table under the sign. He lights a cigarette to go with his after dinner coffee.

Denis is from Sterling, Illinois. He isn't often in Maine.

A second man takes a seat one chair away, a frequent Dysart's customer just stopped in for a generous helping of Daisy Mae bread pudding.

The two men begin talking. Conversation turns to debate over the advantages of the large chain truckstops over the

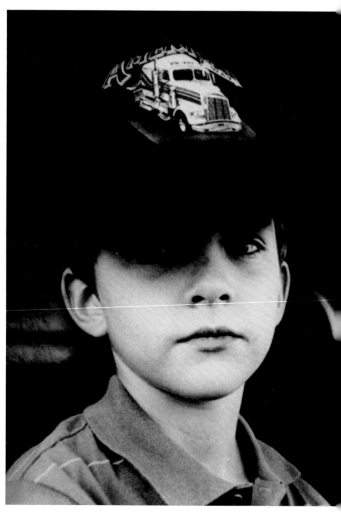

smaller privately owned versions.

"You get down to Ohio where they've got all those Petrol stops. You should see the lounges those places have. Large screen televisions and everything. Not two pinball machines like here.

"Their parking lots will hold a thousand trucks easy. They even send those street cleaners out in the parking lots.

They keep 'em nice and clean," says Dennis.

"Yeah. They may be bigger, " the other trucker responds, "But it's not the same. I can deal with Dave Dysart. If I'm in a bind, he'll help me out. I'm an individual. I'm just one person and I own my truck. It's not just me, I know a lot of the guys.

"It's like a country store compared to a supermarket. Some people just go in to socialize and talk to the people. With a big place, you're in…" He gestures with his fork. "And you're out.

"If you have the money, then you do, if you don't, well?" He shrugs his shoulders as if to imitate the indifferent attitude of the industrial size truckstop.

He takes the last bite of his Daisy Mae pudding, pushes his plate forward, and leans back in his chair. End of conversation. A newcomer joins the table.

"So what's good tonight?"

"You oughta try the Leroy Special." The dessert eater suggests, reaching across the table to point at the

first page of the menu.

"Eighteen scoops of ice cream. It's named after Leroy, ya know. I seen five guys come in here the other day and split one. But now Leroy, I seen him eat the whole thing himself."

By now there is a waitress at the newcomers elbow. "Ready to order? What'll it be?"

Just seconds after taking the order she returns with a basket of thickly sliced home baked bread and a glass of iced tea. Not more than five minutes later she is back again with a large oval platter filled to capacity with what you'd swear to be Mom's home cookin'.

"One thing about it, you don't leave hungry." Chuck Rhoddy remarks as he leaves the restaurant, his ten year old son Jaimie in tow.

"Holidays you can't get near the restaurant. But they always leave one table open just for truckers."

Chuck Rhoddy has been a trucker for 22 years. This summer, Jaimie is riding with him. "I want him to see what it's like." Chuck explains. "Any kid, you know, they see trucks and they want to get up there and take a ride.

"One winter I wanted to take Jaimie with me. So I call up his teacher and ask if he can miss a week of school. Well, I tell ya, he learned more in that week than he ever did in a week of school." Jaimie likes riding with his dad. It gives them time together. He gets to see a lot of different places.

"Once we saw a big convoy. It was really neat," Jaimie says as he plays with a plastic toy truck. Jaimie wears a black t-shirt with a big truck silk-screened on the front. He's got another almost like it in the cab.

"The movies make it [trucking] seem so glamorous. It ain't though. I want Jaimie to see what it's really like," his father explains. "I used to take my daughter with me too. Ever since she was three years old." Chuck smiles to himself, remembering.

"Once this waitress sees me with this three-year old. She can't believe anyone would want to drive around with a three-year old. I did though. She's married now.

"That's my son-in-law's truck right there," he points over his shoulder. "He pulled in right next to me. Never know when you're gonna run into someone you know. Matter of fact we're waiting for him right now. When he's done dinner, we'll leave.

"We're gonna ride together for a while, 'til the next stop. Here he is now…"

Night has fallen on Dysart's. Traffic slows down. A few men linger in the dining room, drinking coffee smoking the day's last cigarette. The crowd that usually fills the doorway has disappeared, leaving empty space and silence. The heavy rumble of engines has stopped. Few trailers sit under the glowing white light of the service islands, and when they pull out, no replacements come.

Music drifts from the open garage door. Spotlights on the back wall silhouette the mechanics in slow motion, putting tools away, getting things in order.

At the edge of the parking lot, small squares of light mark a long row of trucks in the darkness. Truckers relax in their cabs, some reading, some just sitting. Not much but static on the c.b. radio tonight.

"Anyone out there?" a disembodied voice breaks the silence. "Where's everyone tonight?"

A trucker flicks off his c.b. and hits the switch on his dome light as he crawls over the driver's seat into bed. The truckstop looks deserted. Most of the darkened cabs shelter sleeping men.

Their trucks are their homes on the road. Ask any trucker where he sleeps. He'll say "Where else would you go."

Bangor Daily News photo February 16, 2000

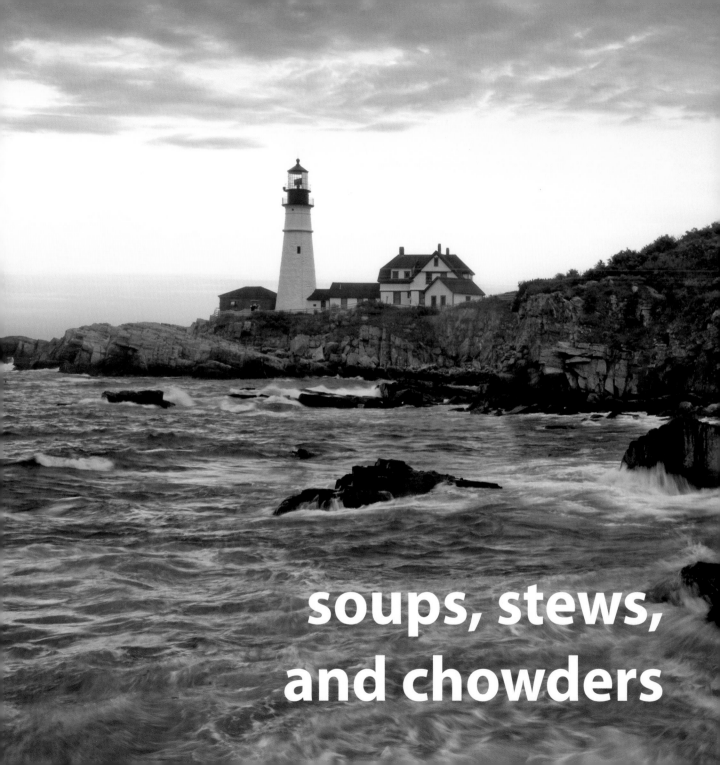

soups, stews, and chowders

We get asked quite frequently on our comment cards, "How did you get that old truck in here?" No, unfortunately there are no trap doors in the building, but one of the sets of windows can be removed and the truck was added to the dining room for appropriate decoration in 1997. It is a 1928 Ford pickup and is now outfitted with wooden racks to display baked goods and gift items.

haddock chowder

1/2 cup butter

1 onion chopped

1 1/2 lbs. haddock

4 oz. of bacon or salt pork, cut into small pieces. (Optional)

3 cups of water

3 cups of diced Maine potatoes (russets or Yukon gold)

3 cups of half and half

salt and pepper to taste

Lighter Load:
1/4 cup of butter
3 cups skim milk
omit bacon/salt pork

Cook the bacon in a large soup pot over medium heat until the bacon or (salt pork) is crisp. Remove the bits and drain on a paper towel for later.

Add onions and butter to the pot and saute until the onions are translucent. This will create a great flavor from the bacon. Add potatoes, haddock, water and salt and pepper. Bring to a boil. Reduce the heat to medium low, and cook, covered, until the potatoes are tender. (about 15 minutes)

Add the half-and-half with salt and pepper to taste. Bring to a simmer over medium heat. At the restaurant we make a larger batch of the base mix (which will store for 3 days) and add the half-and-half when the chowder is ready to serve.

You can top the soup with the bacon or salt pork you set aside earlier for more flavor.

simply

Here's the deal, Mainers take their lobster very seriously. It isn't just a food to us, it's a lifestyle. There are very few places in the world virtually synonymous with a food, but Maine and lobster go hand in hand.

Lobster has economic strength for us as a State, agriculturally, tourism-wise, right down to the millions of lobster-clad t-shirts, postcards, and hats manufactured every year.

A freshly steamed, sweet lobster needs nothing else. And that holds true for those recipes that contain the shelled treasure. Lobster rolls should be mixed just with mayo, and this stew should be made with nothing more than cream and butter.

Those who love lobster, think it is perfect. So why mess with that?

lobster stew

Boil lobsters, remove meat.

Simmer the lobster meat, cut in medium sized pieces, in ½ cup of butter for 10 minutes. Remove from heat and cool slightly.

Slowly add one quart of half and half, stirring constantly. Salt and pepper to taste. Constant stirring gives the stew a rich salmon color.

For the very best flavor the stew should be made 6 hours to 2 days before serving to allow time for aging, the secret of the delicious flavor.

**3 live 1 ¼ lb. lobsters
(or about 1 lb. of lobster meat)**

1/2 cup butter

1 quart of half and half

Lighter Load:
1 quart of milk (whole, 2%, or skim)
1/4 cup of butter instead of ½ cup

Dave's old Michigan

With over 60 acres of property, the majority of it being paved roadways and parking lots, you can imagine what it takes to clean up this place after it snows.

Dave Dysart had, what some might call, an irrational love for plowing snow. Armed with a real life version of dump trucks, little boys only dream of owning, he would get up early and move snow around from dusk till dawn.

Always needing help, both with the workload, and for someone to blame if he happened to hit or damage anything. He would spend hours cleaning up even light dustings. Later in life, when he and his wife would go down to Florida for a few months in the winter, Dave would watch the weather channel to see when the big storms were, and book a flight home to take part in the clean-up.

One time, while Dave was out plowing, a tractor-trailer driver ignored that he had run over and broken an elbow fitting before parking to go into the building to get some lunch. Annoyed at the inconsiderate act, Dave got into his old Michigan front-end loader and scooped up the end of the trailer into the air so the driver couldn't leave without coming to see him to sort out the damages.

There is nothing better after a long day of snow clean-up than a hot, hearty, bowl of beef stew. If you care to brave the roads, come on in for this customer favorite, but follow this recipe and you can have your own to share with fellow shovelers.

beef stew

1 lb. stew beef, cut into 1" cubes

2 cups of baby carrots

1 cup cubed turnip

1 stalk of celery, cut into 1" pieces

1 tsp. gravy master

3 cups beef broth

1 tsp. garlic powder

salt and pepper to taste

2 large Maine potatoes, diced

1 small onion, chopped

Roux

3 tbsp. butter

3 tbsp. flour

Heat 2 tbsp. of oil in a Dutch oven or heavy bottom pot. Cook beef in oil for 15 min., stirring occasionally, until beef is brown. Add hot broth, gravy master and spices.

Heat to boiling; reduce heat to low. Cover and simmer for 2 hours, or until beef is almost tender, add onions and celery, simmer for ½ hour. At this point you add the carrots, potatoes, and turnip and simmer until the vegetables are tender. Thicken with the roux by gradually stirring into beef mixture, stir constantly for 1 minute at a boil; reduce to low heat until thick.

(Thicken with a roux. Roux is made with equal amounts of melted butter and flour blended together until smooth.)

where's Sally?

Since every bill in the restaurant is paid through the front desk cashier, regular diners get to know the cashiers in the front pretty well over the years. Sally, one of the favorite ladies in the front, is known for her love of pot belly pigs and for her incredible ability to not only remember everyone's name she meets, but when she saw you last.

In 2000, Sally took a much-deserved 2-week vacation. To say her absence was noticed would be a complete understatement. Mary Hartt, who filled in for Sally's shifts while she was away, got so tired of answering, "Where's Sally?" that she made a box and slips of paper for people to choose their story. Even though it has been 10 years, Sally still has the fluorescent pink box and it's contents.

Voters were given three options:
1. She's working the strip in NYC
2. She ran away with the pigs
3. She's been committed to rehab

They could also choose to fill in their own story. They ranged from: "She's at a nude beach in Levant", to "She decided to follow her dream of line dancing across America with a pig, a goat, and an ostrich while completely nude and singing the 'Second Week of Deer Camp'".

And then there was the one response that said it all, "I don't know, but the witch is not leaving again for 10 years."

Sal, your ten year wait is up. HR told me that your vacation requests will now be accepted.

In a sauce pan brown hamburger and onions. Drain when done.

Boil the macaroni separately, drain, and set it aside to use later.

In a large soup pot bring broth and remaining ingredients to a boil. Add cooked beef and onions. Let simmer for about 15 minutes. Add the macaroni just before serving to avoid making the macaroni mushy

In the restaurant we use a very thick spaghetti sauce, so you may want to add an additional 2 cups of sauce to your soup.

beef mac soup

3/4 cup diced onions

1 lb. hamburger

1 lb. dry macaroni

2 cups spaghetti sauce

2 1/2 tsp. oregano

2 1/2 tsp. basil

8 cups beef broth

2 dashes of worcestershire sauce

1 or 2 dashes of tabasco sauce

salt and pepper to tast

any day but Tuesday

Because the restaurant is open 24 hours a day, 365 days a year, one of the most important questions on a kitchen job application is "What days are you available to work?" There are a lot of hours in a week that need to be staffed, and the more flexible an applicant is in their schedule, the more appealing they are.

Years ago, a family friend named Jed Cook was hired to be a dishwasher for the summer. When he applied, he marked that he was available at any time on any day, and for the first few weeks he worked his schedule as it was posted.

When his third week rolled around, the young man asked to speak with his manager and informed her that he was now available any day but Tuesday. Thinking it was an odd request, as most teenagers try to get out of working weekend shifts, the manager asked him what conflict he now had on Tuesdays.

"Well it's not really a conflict per se, its just that pea soup is the special on Tuesdays, and I hate to wash the bowls."

pea soup

1 lb. dried split peas

1 chopped onion

1/4 tsp. salt

1/2 tsp. pepper

4 cups water

4 ham bouillon cubes

1 cup ham, cubed

Wash peas and put in a large pot; Add chopped onion, water.

Bring to a boil and then reduce heat. Cover and simmer for 2 hours until peas have broken down and the liquid is reduced.   Add ham and ham bouillon cubes. Simmer for another 1/2 hour. Stir occasionally during simmering to prevent scorching. Season with salt and pepper.

As if the kitchen doesn't have enough to keep them busy, we ask them to prepare a steady supply of fresh, homemade soups all day, everyday. If you come around here often enough, you'll see that there is often a method to our madness and some patterns to the specials board will emerge. Our daily soup offerings are consistently on schedule:

Monday: Corn Chowder
Tuesday: Pea Soup
Wednesday: Turkey Rice (shown here)
Thursday: Beef Mac
Friday: Fish Chowder

Lucky for you, the recipes for all of these soups are right in this book and you can make them whenever the fancy strikes! If you don't feel like cooking, now you know what we will have when you come in.

In a large sauce pan, saute onions, garlic and celery in the vegetable oil over medium heat until tender. Add the remaining ingredients (except rice) to the pot and bring to a boil. When the soup comes to a boil turn down and let simmer until the carrots are tender.

Add the cooked rice, and season with salt and pepper to taste.

turkey rice soup

3 stalks chopped celery

1 tbsp. vegetable oil

1 tbsp chopped garlic

3/4 cup onions

3/4 cup frozen peas (optional)

1 cup sliced carrots

1 tsp. poultry seasoning

1 tsp. tarragon

1/2 tsp. thyme

2 cups turkey meat

8 cups turkey broth

3 cups cooked rice

In the summer, using fresh corn can make this chowder even better. An average ear of corn will yield about 1/2 cup of kernels.

Jane

Jane came to work at Dysart's with young children and retired after putting them though college. For years it was widely known that drivers couldn't drive past Dysart's without coming in to hear what Jane had done lately. There was no telling what she might do and/or say. One of the best stories was about the grumpy driver who sat down and told Jane, "Last time I was in my corn chowder didn't have any corn!"

It was July, fresh corn season, so Jane hurried out to the walk-in and plunked a whole raw husk of corn into a bowl of chowder and served it. The driver's room erupted in laughter and that hungry, grumpy driver left happy.

corn chowder

Very much a regional dish, our corn chowder is seasoned with only salt and pepper. Feel free to add more or less to suit your own taste.

3 tbsp. of butter (or 3 slices of bacon or salt pork are traditional)

4 large potatoes peeled and cubed

2 cups of water

2 medium onions chopped

1 can cream style corn

1 can whole kernel corn

If using salt pork (or bacon,) cut it into small cubes and fry for about 5 minutes. Drain and set aside

salt and pepper to taste

2 ½ cups of half and half *

Melt the butter in a medium soup pot. Add the onions and cook over medium heat, stirring until onions are softened – about six minutes. Add water and potatoes. Bring to a boil, reduce the heat and cook about 10 minutes until almost tender. Add the two cans of corn and seasoning.

Lighter Load:

2 ½ cups of skim milk *

This may be made ahead and stored without the half and half or skim milk. To serve, warm the mixture and add the half and half being careful not to boil.

a true Maine menu

Among the awards and recognition Dysart's has received over the years, one of the ones Mary Hartt is most proud of is winning the state award for the Best Maine Menu in 2003 and 2004. For Hartt, using Maine products is more difficult than using national wholesalers, but it makes a lot of sense.

"Our whole living is because trucks are hauling Maine products through our dooryard, plus, things just taste a lot better when they are fresh," Hartt explained.

Get Real, Get Maine! June 18, 2004

Does it make any difference whether Maine restaurants buy and serve Maine produce? It does to Maine Menus Month 2003 statewide winner, Dysart's restaurant.

And maybe that's why Dysart's is an institution for hungry travelers from all over.

Dysart's started as a truck-stop style restaurant serving hearty homestyle fare 24-hours a day. Dysart's emphasizes traditional home cooking and has built it's reputation on their grandmother's

recipes.

Dysart's is a third generation family operation this started as a truck stop until it was displaced by I-95 in 1957. Ten years later, the landmark opened on 60 acres at exit 180 on Cold Brook Road in Hermon. It offers a traditional Maine menu and complete trucking services.

"Our business was at one time based solely on Maine product hauled on trucks" said co-owner Mary Hartt. "We can tell what season it is by the trucks that are coming through- whether they are hauling potatoes south or bees heading for the blueberry barrens.

Today, Hartt and her brothers Tim and Ed Dysart, feel that in buying local produce, Dysart's supports its customers.

Much of what's on Dysart's menu comes from Maine: clams, scallops, potatoes, blueberries, eggs. Hartt said that some of the beef comes from her father-in-law, Del Hartt's cattle stock.

As a buyer of Maine food items in large quantities, Hartt has noticed an improved effort to grow and deliver produce to restaurant standards and to clearly identify it as being organically grown.

Hartt said, "I want to know I am supporting a Maine business. I'm noticing the "get real. Get Maine!" campaign more, and I think it makes people think about it and want to buy Maine products. And we have our Aroostook county drivers who I'm sure are happy

to know they're eating Maine potatoes," said Hartt.

Dysart's enjoys a loyal following beyond truck drivers. The volume of business exceeds 1,500 meals each weekend day and well over 2,000 on holiday weekends.

On January 7, 2004 at the Blaine House, Governor John Baldacci, First Lady Karen Baldacci, and Agriculture Commissioner Robert Spear recognized Dysart's restaurant (of Hermon, Maine) as the 2003 statewide Maine Menus Month restaurant winner of the "Best Maine Menu" award. Dysart's had the combination of the most votes and high ratings from diners for how well they featured Maine foods on their menu for October (Maine Menus Month) 2003.

Mary Hartt and her brother Tim Dysart (co-owners with their brother Ed Dysart) accepted the award and brought pies and their grandmother's Daisy's bread apple pudding for sampling.

Upon presenting the "Best Maine Menu" plaque to Mary Hartt and Tim Dysart, Governor John E. Baldacci praised the restaurant owners for their restaurant's accomplishments and the commitment to serving local foods over the years.

"Giving this award is easy and a real pleasure, because they really deserve it," he said.

Maine dishes

"why would you want to go and ruin a perfectly good plain potato?"

When Head Chef Shaun Yazbek first started working at the restaurant, it took him a while to adjust his cooking style to what the customers wanted. Shaun's personal tastes include complex seasonings and flavors, so when he added Lyonnaise potatoes (sliced potatoes prepared with onions, garlic, olive oil and parsley) to the specials board, he thought it was a new, but still very basic suggestion.

Later that day, Shaun walked through the building and past the fuel desk where he overheard a trucker talking with one of the attendees there. "What's the deal with these Lion potatoes?" he asked angrily, "why would you want to go and ruin a perfectly good plain potato?"

roast pork

1 boneless pork loin

1 onion

1 cup water

1 tsp. thyme

1 tsp. garlic salt

1 tsp. onion salt

1 tsp. pepper

1 tsp. celery salt

Place pork in a shallow roasting pan. Mix seasonings together, and sprinkle on top of meat. Add water and onion to the bottom of the pan and bake uncovered, at 350 degrees for 30-35 minutes per pound. When you insert a meat thermometer in the center of the roast, make sure it is not touching any bones, and check for 185 degrees.

harvest break

Potatoes are a staple crop in Maine, and have helped define a culture for a large part of Northern Maine for many generations.

Aroostook county produces more potatoes than any other county in the United States. It's also one of the last areas in the country where schools still close down for a yearly "harvest break" to work and help their families get their crops in. While it can be a hard concept to grasp for modern day city folk, this is truly a tradition carried on amongst approximately 380 growers statewide.

Harvest photo courtesy of Green Meadow Farms

country pot roast

4 lb. beef roast

8 small potatoes, halved

8 small onions

8 medium carrots cut into fourths

water

2 tsp. each, salt and pepper

Pot Roast Gravy:

1/2 cup cold water

1/4 cup flour

2 cups broth (taken from your cooked beef and vegetables)

Dysart's serves around 1,500 to 2,000 meals on any given weekend day, and that translates to a lot of potatoes. From home fries with your eggs to the spuds used in this Pot Roast recipe. Dysart's finest potato products come from some of Maine's finest potato farmers.

Currently, the potatoes used in the restaurant come from Green Meadow Farms, the Braley Family Farm, based in Mapleton, Maine. "We feel great about the working relationship that we have with Dysart's. Around here, family businesses need to work together efficiently in order to survive in today's economy," Isaac Braley who co-owns the family farm with his father Glendon.

Cook beef in a heavy bottomed pot or Dutch oven until brown on all sides. Reduce heat to low and sprinkle with salt and pepper.

Cover the meat with water and bring it to a boil. Reduce heat to low. Cover and simmer for 2 ½ hours. Add vegetables, simmer for another hour or until beef is tender (200 degrees internal) and vegetables are done.

To make the gravy: Remove the vegetables and beef from your pot. Skim the fat from the surface and discard. Whisk together 1/4 cup of flour and 1/2 cup of cold water in a bowl until smooth. Bring 2 cups of the beef broth to a boil, and slowly whisk in your flour mixture. Simmer until thickened.

roast turkey

**a thawed turkey
(1-2 lbs. per person)**

1 tsp. salt

1/2 tsp. pepper

1 tsp. garlic powder

potato stuffing

2 cups hot mashed potatoes

2 cups bread cubes

1/2 tsp. pepper

1/2 tsp. salt

1 tbsp. poultry seasoning

1/2 cup butter

1/2 cup diced onion

1 cup diced celery

1 cup turkey broth

In the restaurant we cook our stuffing separate from the turkey. If you are using a frozen turkey, make sure it is completely thawed (this can take up to a few days depending on the size of the bird). Season the outside of your turkey with salt, pepper, and garlic powder.

Place turkey, breast side up, in an open roasting pan and cover lightly with a tent of foil to prevent the bird from browning too rapidly during roasting. Do not add water. Bake at 325 degrees for 3 1/2 to 4 hours, until internal temperature of turkey reaches 180 degrees. Remove foil during last 45 minutes to brown turkey.

Stuffing: Melt butter in a frying pan. Add celery and onion, cook until tender. Combine with the bread cubes and other ingredients. Mix well. For a moist stuffing, mix in lightly, enough stock to moisten the bread.

If you are baking the stuffing outside of the bird, place it in a casserole dish and bake at 350, covered, for about an hour.

holy cow

When one local diner was asked what three foods he associated with Dysart's he answered, "Eggs with beans, poutine, and those huge ice cream puff things." Okay, so not everyone thinks of Dysart's when they are in the mood for a cut of prime rib, but with the meat for all of the restaurant's beef products coming from a farm 18 miles down the road, you couldn't ask for fresher or more local beef.

Delmont Hartt, went to a cow auction in 1976 and ended up buying a few beef cows. Although he smirks and blames the original purchase on his dear wife Sheila, he loves those cows and what was once a hobby became a significant part of his life. Since then, he has owned as many as 150 and is the primary beef supplier to the restaurant.

Sold by the "live pound", an average beef cow weighs around 1400 pounds and is taken to Gray, Maine to become the freshest ground beef and steaks you will find in any restaurant.

smothered beef

When you are using beef in your recipes, the quality of meat is key and we encourage you to buy the best you can to make the difference in your cooking.

1 lb. stew beef

2 cups onion, sliced

1/2 cup flour

2 tbsp. cooking oil

1 tsp. garlic salt

1 tsp. pepper

1 tsp. onion salt

1 tsp. celery salt

Trim all fat from stew beef and cut in one inch cubes. Coat the meat with flour, salt and pepper. Place the meat in a heavy pot or Dutch oven for braising. Brown on all sides in the hot oil. Add other spices.

Cover with water, and cook at a low/medium heat until meat is tender. (2 to 2 1/2 hours) Add the onions and cover for the last 1/2 hour to cook down to a rich thickness.

special for daddy

Dave Dysart, who failed many taste tests to determine if he could actually tell the difference, didn't think bread tasted as good if the kitchen used mixers. Because of this strong belief, every loaf of bread sold here was made completely by hand until 1992. Now a days, mixers are used to combine ingredients, but final kneading and forming the bread is still done by hand.

"Little Timmy" (Tim Dysart, who is now in his forties) used to go out back while the bakers were making bread and ask for a small ball of dough. He would carry it around all day in his little, grubby hands, rolling and kneading it on various surfaces. Then, at the end of the day he would add various creative ingredients (raisins, licorice, whatever) and bake it special to give to his Daddy for a snack.

Technology and modernization have transformed nearly every kitchen across America, but many things around here are still done "the way they should be". This boiled dinner and red flannel hash, are two examples of traditional Maine food, that is and always will be prepared from scratch with great care to preserve their authenticity.

We can also promise that there are no little, grubby hands in the kitchen.

boiled dinner

2 lbs. well-trimmed corned beef brisket

3 cups baby carrots

6 small onions

1 turnip, cubed

3 potatoes, cut in half

1 small head of cabbage, quartered

1 small can whole beets

1 tbsp. pickling spice

Boiled Dinner:
Place corned beef in Dutch oven (or large heavy pot) and cover with water. Add pickling spices. Simmer for 3 hours. Add the all the vegetables and simmer for another 60 minutes. Remove beef to warm platter, and keep warm.

This can also be cooked in a crock pot. Add all ingredients and cook on low heat for 6-8 hours. Traditional boiled dinners are served with a side of beets.

Red Flannel Hash:
Heat butter in a large skillet (preferably cast iron) cast iron pan is traditional. Add all the ingredients except the beets. When everything is chopped and heated add the beets.

Heat slowly, chopping all the ingredients as they cook. When everything is chopped and heated add the beets. Serve warm.

red flannel hash

2 cups corned beef

2 cups left over potatoes

2 cups left over cabbage

2 cups left over carrots

2 cooked onions

1 can of sliced beets

2 tbsp. vegetable oil or butter

some things never change

Let's face it, the Bangor area shuts down at a pretty early hour, leaving the young people here little to do. Dysart's has become a night time hang out for many locals, and if you ask someone who grew up here, their stories are endless.

One Hampden native, Jessica, remembers that one of her favorite Dysart's memories was after her high school won the Eastern Maine Skiing Championship and the team decided to come in for a girls vs. boys competition over who could eat the 18 wheeler the fastest. For those of you who don't know, the 18 wheeler is a delicious mess of a sundae comprised of 18 scoops of ice cream and every topping you can imagine. The way she remembers it, the girls won the competition despite being out numbered by their male competitors.

Even when she wasn't here with an organized group, Jess and her friends would often congregate at one of the long tables. "If we had, say, an 11:00 curfew, there wasn't a whole lot else to do. Oh, those poor waitresses though- send them an apology for me. We had no money to tip as well as we should have, and we never seemed to be able to leave without my friend Chad accidentally tipping over at least one water pitcher. Dysart's was a significant part of growing up for kids around here, we were lucky they didn't ban all of us."

Jess thinks back to the items the group would order most. "Egg McRuth's were a big one, and pancakes. There was novelty in being able to get breakfast at nighttime. And for whatever reason, I remember one kid always getting Shepherd's Pie from the Thursday specials menu."

There will always be new generations of high schoolers knocking over our water pitchers, and Shepherd's Pie is still on the specials board every Thursday.

Some things never change.

shepherd's pie

1 lb. ground beef

4 cups hot, seasoned mashed potatoes

1 large onion, diced

1 12oz. can whole kernel corn

1 12oz. can creamed corn

3 tbsp. margarine

Sauté onion and ground beef in margarine until beef is brown and onions are translucent. Drain away excess fat. Layer this on the bottom, add the two types of corn for the next layer and top with the mashed potatoes. Bake until the top of the potatoes are starting to brown, about 30 minutes.
Serve immediately.

saturday nights and baked beans

Here in Maine, we have our rituals. In the summer we have our state fairs. In the winter we have ice fishing and snowmobiling. In the springtime, we have various home & garden shows around the state. In August we have the Folk Festival in Bangor. In July we have the Lobster Festival in Rockland. Perhaps, though one of the best-known rituals we have in Maine is Saturday night beans and franks.

Whether you're baking beans at home or attending a church or civic organization supper, if the event is on Saturday night, you can almost guarantee that baked beans will be on the menu. Sometimes people serve them with brown bread, sometimes with dinner rolls, and sometimes even with cole slaw. But whatever the side dish, the baked beans themselves are always the mainstay of the Saturday night meal.

At my parents' home growing up, I always knew that Saturday meant baked beans. Now, my dad kinda cheated. You see, technically baked beans are supposed to be just that: baked. My dad decided that an easier way for him would be to put them in the slow-cooker. So, on Friday, he'd soak the beans overnight. Then on Saturday morning, he'd combine all the ingredients and set the slow-cooker on low. The beans would remain on low all day and by dinner time, they'd be ready.

Here at Dysart's, well, we have baked beans on the menu all the time (yup, that's right, 24 hours a day, 7 days a week--because after all, baked beans with breakfast is another Maine thing!) Saturday Night still holds a special place with us. When you come in to visit us on Saturday nights take a look at our special boards on the walls. Without fail, you will see Saturday Night Beans and Franks listed as one of the day's specials. And so, with that being said, we want to share with you our baked beans recipe. We hope that you will enjoy it--and when Saturday night rolls around we hope that this Maine ritual will become your own with Saturday Night Beans & Franks. Enjoy!   -Lee Davis

Our beans come from East Corinth, Maine

Preheat the oven to 250 degrees. In a large covered pot add soaked beans and remaining ingredients, with enough water to cover beans; Bake for about 8 hours. Check beans periodically to make sure they do not need water. If water is needed, add enough boiling water to cover the beans again.
Experienced cooks say the beans use more water when it is going to rain.

Maine baked beans

1 lb. yellow-eye beans, soaked overnight

1 large onion

1/4 lb. salt pork

1 tbsp. salt

1/2 tsp. white pepper

1/4 cup brown sugar

2 tbsp. dry mustard

1/2 cup molasses

1967
PRESENT LOCATION

This is a photo of the current building when it was first built in 1967. Many changes and additions have been made since then as the business evolved and expanded.

turkey pot pie

2 1/2 cups cut up chicken or turkey, cooked and cooled

1 package frozen peas

2 cups carrots

3 cups turkey broth

1/3 cup flour

1/3 cup melted margarine

1/3 cup diced onion

1 cup milk

salt and pepper to taste

Pre-heat your oven to 425 degrees.
Melt margarine in 2-quart saucepan over medium heat with onion, salt, and pepper. Cook, stirring constantly until onions are soft; remove from heat. Stir in broth, carrots and turkey. Bring mixture to a boil. Boil until carrots are cooked, about 10 minutes.

To thicken; Stir milk and flour together until smooth. Slowly pour into the cooking broth to thicken. Add peas.

At Dysart's we put the 'pies' into individual ramekins and bake with a puff pastry on top for 15 minutes.

Variation; Serve as a shortcake. Place turkey mix over homemade biscuits.

Note: This will freeze well and make a nice quick meal on nights where time is short.

behind the scenes in the kitchen

From one of the 230 seats in any of the three dining rooms, a hungry customer can see little more of the kitchen than bustling feet, swinging doors, and servers easily carrying armfuls of carefully balanced plates. But what it takes to pump out over 1,500 meals each day, all day, might surprise even the most experienced restaurant go-er.

While the kitchen is staffed around the clock, one might say that the bakers (who arrive at 4:00 in the morning) officially start the day. Between baking an average of 7 batches of homemade bread (roughly 240 giant loaves) each morning, and what it takes to offer an average of 25 dessert options daily, they are kept busy.

Then there is the grill. Manned by six cooks on a busy day, they are capable of filling orders from Fisherman's Platters, to Poutine, to almost an entire separate breakfast menu (waffles and biscuits & gravy are not served after 11am).

Pushing out plates often marked by different colored picks signifying ingredients omitted, how things are cooked, or varieties of omelets, the cooks are the driving force behind what's on your plate.

There is a symbiotic relationship between the kitchen and the servers, filled with respect and tension.

"Sometimes it's a little like a UFC fight in here. We come in to work friends, have a few major grapples throughout a shift, but leave most of the head-butting on the kitchen floor when we punch out to go home," explained Rollie Partridge, a supervisor from 'team kitchen staff'.

But the food on your plate is not finished when it is placed in the 8 foot "window" for the waitresses to pick up. Many things on your plate come not from the back kitchen, but from the front where waitresses put the finishing touches on many menu items. From making their own salads, portioning off beans, coleslaw and other sides, to plating and preparing all dessert items, it's not all about table-side manner.

While it has been said that it takes a village to raise a child, it could be argued that it takes an army to feed a truck stop. An army, and 11 refrigeration units, 9 industrial-sized ovens, 12 fryolaters, 2 dishwashers using 50 gallons of water an hour, and very comfortable shoes.

Kitchen Lingo

What's it wearing? : What side dishes go with it?
Mardi Gras : Mashed potatoes with gravy
86 on ___ : We're out of it
Scoobie Snacks : A mistake that the servers can eat
Sand Bagged : When the kitchen gets a bunch of large orders all at one time
Double Parked : A server has two full orders that need to be delivered sitting in the window
Seafood on Wheat : A hot chick in the dining room

"Sometimes it's a little like a UFC fight in here. We come in to work friends, have a few major grapples throughout a shift, but leave most of the head-butting on the kitchen floor when we punch out to go home"

fish and seafood

"from away"

Matt left Bangor, headed south to attend Texas A&M University, with pure excitement about the new experiences ahead of him. Although he was born out of state, Matt is a Mainer at heart, and this became even more true as he started his life in the south.

It was around that first holiday break from college when Matt realized that all of the Texas BBQ in the world couldn't replace the simple tastes of Maine foods. It was only appropriate that the first time he and his high school friends were all reunited after that first semester, it was at Dysart's. Some missed the fried seafood, for some it was the ice cream pies, but for all of the friends, being back together eating from the same menu brought back a feeling of home.

Matt still enjoys living in Texas, but when he makes it home for a visit, Dysart's is always on the itinerary. Lobster rolls are a seasonal item to the menu here, so although he couldn't order them over those winter semester breaks, he looks forward to them on his summer visits.

Lobster rolls must be totally pristine and simple. When you are a Mainer-you can tell who is "from away" because they put "things" in their lobster roll. The classic Maine roll is lobster mixed with mayonnaise - and layered over chopped lettuce on a grilled hotdog bun.

In the restaurant we grill the hot-dog buns when the order comes in. We keep the lobster cold until the moment the server is ready to deliver the food because nothing is better than cold lobster salad in a warm hotdog bun.

lobster rolls

2 cups of cooked lobster, cut into chunks

1/2 cup of mayonnaise (more if needed)

Toss the lobster with the mayonnaise. Keep chilled.

4 conventional hot dog buns

3 tbsp. butter

Heat a frying pan to medium heat. Brush the hot-dog rolls with butter on both sides until golden brown. Fill the rolls with a layer of lettuce and 1/4 of the lobster meat. Serve immediately.

fried clams, "as good as any"

The Washington Post   June 19, 1985   Written by: Bob Kelleter

Several years ago at the Maine State Society's annual lobster dinner, I won a door prize- a letter redeemable for a free dinner for two at Dysart's truck stop just off interstate 95 on Cold Brook Road (exit 42) in Hermon, Maine.

I figured I'd rather keep the letter (you can imagine the laughs it gets) than eat the dinner and didn't bother going to Dysart's (which would have been a 700-mile trip from here). Then, last year I was in a group looking for a bite on Sunday night in Bangor and the only place we could find open in the greater metropolitan area was Dysart's.

I didn't have the letter along (I keep it at home in a safe place), but Dysart's was still worth the wait- and full fare. The fried-clam plate ("It's one of our specials," says Dave Dysart) was as good as any I've ever had (fried clams are almost always good, unless they're cooked in batter and then they're always bad). Perhaps, they were even a match for those that Rita served at her clam shack in Bar Harbor (and anyone who was there knows how great they were) in the early '60's.

But Rita couldn't serve on rainy days. Her shack was only big enough for a refrigerator, the fryer, and Rita (who was rather hefty), so the patrons stood outside or sat on stools at the counter.

Dysart's, on the other hand, is almost always open (the pumps are never off, but the restaurant does close for 12 hours on Christmas), has seating under roof for 112, a parking lot with room for as many as 250 rigs, a bank of 12 pay phones and delicious chocolate cream pie (although the clam plate is so large that dessert is work). Rita never had pie.

Prepare a 'wash', page 94

With bowls large enough to dip your fry basket, prepare 2 cups of dry clam fry mix in one bowl and the wash in the other.

This next step is what we call, "Wet, dry, wet, dry." This means using a wire basket and dipping about a fourth of the clams in the wet wash (let drain) and then the dry clam fry, return it to the wet wash. On the last "dry", dip again into the clam fry.

Test the deep fryer to be at 375°F and fry the clams for about 30 seconds (they burn fast) or until golden brown. Drain on paper towels.

fried clams

1 pint shucked clams, rinsed and well drained

4 cups of clam fry mix

2 cups of water (for the wash)

oil (for deep frying)

tartar sauce, for dipping

"I asked Dysart how this great truckstop began. Dysart is a huge man, built like a truck. He stands over six feet three inches, weighs over 250 pounds. He smiles a lot, moves and talks quietly.

He loves trucks, now owns half a dozen big rigs himself and eagerly inspects the details of every new model which comes onto his 11 acre apron."

Bill Caldwell, Maine Sunday Telegram
February 20, 1972

In the restaurant we call the wet seafood dip a "wash". The wash is made with a 50 – 50 blend of clam fry and water.

Mix together 2 cups of water and 2 cups of clam fry mix in a bowl big enough for your deep fry basket to fit. This will make the wash.

With bowls large enough to dip your fry basket prepare the remaining 2 cups of clam fry mix in one bowl and the 2 cups of panko in the other.

panko fried shrimp

1 lb. shelled Maine shrimp

4 cups clam fry mix

2 cups water

2 cups Panko (for breading)

Using a wire basket, dip about a third of the shrimp in the wash, letting the excess liquid drain off.

This next step is what we call, "Wet, dry, wet, dry." This means dip the shrimp in the wet wash (let drain) and then the dry clam fry, return it to the wet wash. On the last "dry" dip in the panko.

Test the deep fryer to be at 375 and fry the shrimp until golden brown for about 2 minutes. Serve with cocktail sauce.

fine (truckstop) china

Grandmother Daisy Dysart was a delicate housewife who spent her time looking proper and was an active participant of garden club and other societal groups. She would dab the corners of her mouth and cross her legs at the ankles, like a good woman should.

With all of the things that needed to be handled when the business was first opening, Daisy was put in charge of choosing the plates and silverware that would be used at the restaurant. Knowing nothing about the restaurant world, she chose very lovely china to accompany the carpeted dining room, and aspired to run one of Bangor's finest dining establishments.

One of the many things Daisy hadn't thought through when making her plate selection, were that these dishes would be washed in mass quantities by dish washers who seem capable of shattering plastic. Not accustomed to such rough and tumble washing habits, she was astonished as her plates disappeared day after day. It wasn't long before the kitchen was scrambling to find usable, clean, plates and before Daisy took the remainder of the dishes home with her to host the garden club.

A few dishes still remain and are kept at the Dysart family camp. One is shown here, and we hope you get a laugh at the thought of your next order of fried haddock coming out of our kitchen on this fine china.

Prepare a 'wash', page 94

With bowls large enough to dip your fry basket prepare 2 cups of dry clam fry mix in one bowl and the wash in the other

This next step is what we call, "Wet, dry, wet, dry." This means using a wire basket dip a piece of haddock in the wet wash (let drain) and then the dry clam fry mix, return it to the wet wash. On the last "dry" dip again into the clam fry.

Test the deep fryer to be at 375F and fry the haddock for about 3 minutes (depending on the thickness) or until golden brown. Drain on paper towels. Enjoy with tartar sauce.

fried haddock

1 lb. of haddock
rinsed and well drained

4 cups of clam fry mix

2 cups of water (for the wash)

oil (for deep frying)

tartar sauce, for dipping

smiling at us

Since so many of our employees have been here for so long, they all understand that it is the little things that make coming to work enjoyable, and that things are much happier if you create a "work family". For this reason, communication is encouraged and common between people on different shifts and through all levels of management. Comments and suggestions left in the suggestion box (located on the "cookie truck" in the main dining room) are shared, as are stories collected. As you might imagine with some of the characters that pass through our doors, stories can cover a broad spectrum. Here is one a front desk cashier sent along as an FYI to management:

"A customer called to see if we had found his new set of false teeth that he took out while eating and left in a napkin. We looked through the small bag of trash, and of course they were not in there. I spotted another bag, opened it up and they were sitting right on top of the trash almost smiling at us! I called him and he is picking them up later at the fuel desk, so there they sit, wrapped in another napkin, waiting for their mouth."

baked stuffed scallops

1 1/2 lbs. scallops

4 tbsp. butter

seafood stuffing

seafood stuffing

2 oz. scallops

2 oz. haddock

2 oz. shrimp

2 oz. lobster

8 oz. butter

10 oz. Ritz crackers

dash parsley

Divide scallops in 4 ramekins, top with 1 tbsp. of butter each, and bake for 10 minutes at 350 (save 2 oz. of scallops for the stuffing).

Sauté 2 oz. each of scallops, haddock, shrimp, and lobster in butter for approximately 8-10 minutes or until cooked. When cooked add ritz crackers and mix thoroughly. Add some parsley for color.

Remove ramekins from oven and add seafood stuffing on top of your scallops, place them back in the oven for an additional 10 minutes.

You can make the stuffing a day ahead if you like. If you do so, keep in mind, if the stuffing is cold when you put it on top of the haddock filet, you'll need to cook the dish a little longer, about 15 minutes to get it warmed through.

forgotten tip

One of the first things waitstaff learn around here are the differences in tipping between some of our customers. Without getting into the reasoning or the arguments about which tipping standard is the "right" one, lets chalk it up to a cultural difference and get on with the story.

The day after I earned my green apron, signifying that I was no longer a "trainee" (trainees wear a maroon apron, with white embroidering labeling that they are in training), I got my first large group of customers filling every seat in my section. There were 22 of them, all on Harleys, driving through to Laconia, and boy did I pamper that group.

"Oh, let's find a place to store your helmets so they aren't in your way." "Here, I got water ready for everyone when I saw you walk in, and there is a menu at every seat." "Oh sure, I will send orders to the kitchen depending on how long they take to cook so you all get your food at the same time.""Does everyone want more free rolls?"

They each wanted separate checks, and with all of them ordering Baked Stuffed Lobster, Fisherman Platters, and the like, I couldn't help but mentally computer my tip while they sat for 2.5 hours (that's almost a week in truckstop time) and enjoyed their appetizers, meals, desserts, and multiple beverages. When all was said and done, the bills totalled $622.83. Yes, after 6 years, I still remember.

I was nearly in tears when one man decided he was going to pay for everyone's meals and left without leaving me any tip at all. I was red with frustration, cleaning up the piles of plates and trash when I looked up, and there is the check-payer, smiling and walking towards me.

"I almost forgot something" he declared, and my hand instinctively reached out for the cash tip I was so hopeful for. He ducked to my right, and reached out behind me, where his helmet was laying in my accommodating hiding place. "Can't get far without this." he said.

Saute scallops, butter and wine/chicken stock together for 3 or 4 min. or until scallops are lightly browned. Put into 2 or 3 ramekins (oven safe dish) and top with crushed Ritz crackers, drizzle with honey and bake for 15 minutes at 350.

legendary scallops

1 lb. scallops

4 oz. honey

4 tbsp. butter

1 cup crushed ritz crackers

4 oz. wine or chicken stock

nostalgia with two side dishes

I had never heard of Finnan Haddie when the recipe came across my desk at the beginning of this book-making process, I thought it was just a cutesy name for some broiled fish dish. Once I asked around, everyone had something to pipe in about it.

The cooks can't stand the smell of the kitchen when they prepare it, the servers can't believe anyone would actually order it, and the customers eat it right up. Everyone who sees it on the menu shares their memories of the old days, when so and so used to always make it for such and such a time.

Judy Knight, restaurant manager, remembers when Dave Dysart first added Finnan Haddie to the menu 15 or so years ago. Never having cooked a day in his life, he knew how he liked things to taste (just like his mom made it), but never put much thought into how labor intensive something would be to make.

"He wanted us to cover the smoked fish with milk, scald it, and pour it off. And repeat this three times. That took an hour- certainly not feasible in a restaurant setting," explained Knight. She added that he also refused any seasonings in the dish because his personal tastes were just plain food.

If you love this dish, you will love the way our cooks prepare it and we encourage you to make it at home. Just a word of advice: keep the air freshener handy.

finnan haddie

1 1/2 lbs. smoked haddock

2 1/2 cups milk

Place finnan haddie into a large sauce pan and cover with milk, soak for about one hour. After one hour, bring to a gentle boil (still in milk) over medium high heat.

egg sauce:

Reduce to low and simmer. Take care not to burn milk. (10 - 15 minutes).

recipe page 105

When serving, cover with hot egg sauce (recipe on page 105).

While the use of GPS and cell phones has greatly reduced the number of truckers relying on CB radio as a primary means of communication, there are still many year's worth of radio jargon contributing to conversations that are completely meaningless to the untrained ear.

Alligator: piece of tire in the road

Antler alley: anywhere with deer or moose crossing signs

Barbershop: a bridge lower than 13' 6" (standard minimum height on all Interstates and state highway systems) that could scrape off the top portions of a tractor-trailer rig.

Bobtail: a tractor without a trailer.

Bumper sticker: a car riding too close behind a truck

Dandruff: light snow

Double-nickel: 55 mph (90km/hr)

Eighty-eights: loves and kisses

Lot lizard: a prostitute that frequents truck stops

Meat wagon: ambulance

Piggy bank: a toll plaza

Plain wrapper: unmarked law enforcement vehicle

Seat cover: female passenger

The zipper: the dashed lane markings

Sailboating: running low on fuel

salmon pie

1 pound of salmon (1 oz., pieces)

3 puff pastry shells

egg sauce

1 cup half & half

1 tsp. pepper

1 tsp. salt

1 bouillon cube

2 or 3 eggs hard boiled

roux

3 tbsp. butter

3 tbsp. flour

Short cut to an egg sauce - keep a roux (butter paste) in a jar in refrigerator. Roux is make with equal amounts of melted butter and flour blended together.

In 3 ramekins place the salmon pieces. Cover with the egg sauce. Place puff pastry on the top. Bake in the oven at 350 degrees for 15 minutes or until crust is done.

To make egg sauce: heat the milk and bouillon to a boil over low heat. Whisk in the roux. Add seasonings. Stir constantly until mixture boils for 1 min. Remove from heat. If the sauce is too thick, stir in more cream or milk.

desserts

Betty

You'll hear Betty Feeney's name throughout this book, because for so many years she became friends and family with almost everyone in the Dysart's community. I met with Betty in Dysart's hair salon, just on the other side of the fuel desk when she was in for a "permanent". Always wanting her hair just so, she agreed to answer some questions but would, "certainly not have her photo taken". With so many memories, and the humility to not think any of them were too special, it took a while to warm her up.

Betty is a woman who swears that WD-40 helps ease the pain of the arthritis in her hands. When she first came to Dysart's with her late husband Greg, she was the restaurant baker. Regardless of how delicious her baked goods were, and how much she loved making the various pies, after a few months Betty asked if she could train to be a line cook. "After a hard days work, and full bakers racks of desserts, I would come in the next morning and it would all be gone. Boy, was that hard!"

Peel, core and slice apples into a 9 x 13 buttered pan until 3/4 full. Sprinkle the apples with lemon juice. Pour 1/2 cup of water over this mixture.

Mix binder ingredients together in a large bowl. Pour the binder over the top of the apples. Mix together a little.

Place all the ingredients for the topping, except butter, into a bowl. Mix very well. Melt the butter and pour into the dry ingredients. This will take time to mix in. Continue to work together (works best if you use your fingertips) until it looks like crumbs. Spread evenly over the apples in a second layer. Once you have it even press down.

Place the pan onto a cookie sheet (prevents a mess). Bake at 350 degrees for about 45 minutes. Check the apples with a fork to see if tender.

apple crisp

8-10 cups peeled, sliced apples

1 tbsp. lemon juice

Topping:

1 cups flour

1 1/2 cups rolled oats

1 1/2 cups brown sugar

1 tsp. salt

1 tsp. nutmeg

1 tbsp. cinnamon

3/4 cup butter

Binder:

1/2 cup sugar

1 tbsp. flour

2 tsp cinnamon

a small taste of summer

In the Dysart's kitchen, crisps (like this strawberry-rhubarb one) are made in motel pans that each make approximately 30 servings. When they are ready to be served, they are placed in a large refrigerator in the front kitchen where waitstaff use an oversized scoop to portion out the dessert, and top it with ice cream if the customer wants it.

The delicious aroma of this sweet and tangy dessert wafts into the faces of each person who opens that fridge. Never mind the sight of it bubbling after being warmed, or the slowly melting Gifford's ice cream when the scoop is first placed on top.

Since I am writing this anonymously , lets just say that not burying my face into the pan for a taste each and every time I served it was one of the hardest parts of my job as a Dysart's waitress.

Lets also say, that there is a strong possibility that the occasional attempt was made to "level out the pan", which may or may not have involved "excess" coming from the pan and into a small portion cup.

At this point, I may or may not have scurried off to a corner to savor the small taste of summer and the memories that came of my grandmother baking this dessert when I was a little girl. I feel a little guilty saying it because my "Ma"meant the world to me, but her recipe had nothing on this treat of all treats.

I wonder if that pan needs to be cleaned up a little bit right now?

strawberry rhubarb
or
bumbleberry crisp

4 cups rhubarb (1/2 inch pieces)

4 cups strawberries

Topping:

1 cup flour

1 1/2 cups rolled oats

1 1/2 cups brown sugar

1 tsp. salt

1 tsp. nutmeg

1 tbsp. cinnamon

3/4 cup butter

Binder:

1 cups sugar

1 tbsp. flour

2 tsp cinnamon

1 tbsp. cornstarch

Mix binder ingredients together in a bowl. Pour the binder over the top of the apples. Mix together a little.

Place all the ingredients for the topping except butter into a bowl. Mix very well. Melt the butter and pour into the dry ingredients. This will take time to mix in. Continue to work together (works best if you use your fingertips) until it looks like crumbs. Spread evenly over the fruit in a second layer. Once you have it even press down.

Place the pan onto a cookie sheet (Prevents a mess) . Bake at 350 degrees for about 3/4 hour. Check the apples with a fork to see if tender.

Bumbleberry Crisp: Use half blueberries and half raspberries to make your 8 cups. Follow the remaining recipe and ingredients.

Mrs. Daisy Dysart

Today along the U.S. highways and interstates, Truck Stop dining mostly consists of fast food chains. Dysart's is almost a dinosaur in the Truck Stop world because we serve homemade food. Whether you're having one of our delicious soups or a slice of warm bread—our food is homemade with you in mind. At Dysart's you know you can still follow the age-old philosophy of: "If the truckers go there to eat, it must be good."

Daisy reading with her great grandson Dale Hartt

During the first year that Dysart's was open, tons of homemade bread heels were thrown away. Daisy Dysart suggested we make her Bread Pudding recipe to put the bread heels to use. The secret ingredient in her recipe is apples. We serve other bread puddings seasonally, but our Daisy Apple Bread Pudding is served every day because it is Daisy – the best.

Although others may vote for Dysart's homemade bread, muffins or biscuits, Del Hartt, a customer since 1967, believes the restaurant is best known for its Daisy Apple Bread Pudding. He jokes when he comes in that he "taste-checks the pudding" so we don't mess with it. It is served hot, and topped with vanilla ice cream.

Daisy bread apple pudding

4 cups soft bread, cubed

1 cup sugar

1 tsp. vanilla

2 tsp. cinnamon

1 1/2 cups milk

3 eggs

1 cup thinly sliced apples

1/2 cup raisins

Loosely fill a glass or metal 9 x 13 baking dish with your bread. Pour 1/2 cup hot water over the bread and sprinkle top of wet bread with cinnamon. In a large mixing bowl beat together sugar, eggs, milk, and vanilla.

Fold apples and raisins in the mixing bowl and pour over bread mixture. Stir gently. Bake for one hour at 350º.

hasty pudding

People who haven't had this dish before often ask 'What is that brown stuff?' and that's because, quite frankly, Indian Pudding is one of the ugliest desserts out there. But with one taste of the sweet molasses flavor, many are surprised by how much they enjoy this traditional dish.

Despite the title, early New England settlers did not adapt this recipe from Native Americans. "Indian" refers to the 'Indian meal' used – or cornmeal as we call it today, as wheat flour wasn't available.

Originally cooked in a pot over the open hearth, the pudding was very dense. No, we don't build a campfire out back to cook our pudding, but we have kept the traditional spices and flavors. If you come into the restaurant in November, you can sample this historic dessert. Beware to those who don't love their sweets sweet, as this dish has an extremely rich flavor, and is served with ice cream or homemade whipped cream.

Fun fact: This dessert is referred to as Hasty Pudding in the Yankee Doodle tune for children. "... And there we saw the men and boys, as thick as hasty pudding."

indian pudding

4 cups milk

2 eggs

1/2 cup molasses

3/4 cup cornmeal

1/2 cups sugar

1 tsp. ginger

3/4 tsp. nutmeg

1 tsp. cinnamon

1 tsp. salt

1 tsp. vanilla

In a bowl mix together cornmeal, sugar, ginger, nutmeg, cinnamon, and salt with 2 cups of cold milk. Mix well.

In medium sized sauce pan heat 2 cups of milk to just before it starts to boil. Stir in the molasses and heat back up to boiling point. Once gently boiling, slowly add in the cornmeal mixture from above. Mix very well all the time you are adding to prevent lumps

You need to heat the mixture back to boiling, and stir until the mixture starts to thicken.

Once mixture starts to thicken you need to temper the eggs. Beat the eggs in a separate bowl, and take about 1 cup of the hot liquid from the pan and mix it into the eggs. If you skip this step, the eggs will heat too quickly, and you will end up with scrambled eggs in your pudding.

After they have been tempered, add the eggs to the rest of the mixture on the stove. Cook for about a minute, and remove from heat. Add the vanilla and pour the whole mixture into a 9 x 13 pan. Let cool to room temperature and then refrigerate. The pudding will thicken as it cools.

they always come back

Dysart's is lucky to have kept many of the best, reliable, long-time waitstaff for years and years. There is always a familiar face, and much less turnover than other establishments. Still, there are always those who come and go. The fall is a particular time for change, many employees leave their aprons behind to go begin college life.

Not surprisingly, during their time here they have developed a taste for their favorite food. When they are back in town they inevitably return for a little sample of their favorite Dysart's guilty pleasure.

Several years ago, there was a server working here named Alan. (Hi Alan!) During his time with us, he found that he LOVED our blueberry cobbler. Hot or cold, small bite or bowlful, Alan was hooked. Cobbler isn't something you can find on every restaurant menu, and Dysart's has had years to tweak the recipe to just how Alan liked it. Alas, after working a summer's worth of late-night shifts, Alan went off to college.

After saying our goodbyes and good lucks, it wasn't too long before fall break and we had a visit from Alan who just needed some cobbler. We soon came to expect to see Alan visiting over school vacations and summers, and to this day we get the occasional call from him to make sure it is available when he comes in.

blueberry cobbler

Filling:

4 cups blueberries

1 tsp. lemon juice

1 tbsp. water

1/2 cup sugar

2 tbsp. flour

1 tbsp. corn starch

1/2 tsp. cinnamon

Topping:

1 cups flour

2 tbsp. sugar

1/2 tbsp. baking powder

1/2 tsp. salt

3 tbsp. butter

1/2 cup milk

1 cup milk

Stir together sugar and cornstarch in a small saucepan. Add berries, lemon juice and water. Cook, stirring constantly, until mixture thickens and boils. Boil and stir 1 minute. Pour into a 2 quart casserole dish.

In a separate bowl stir together the ingredients for the topping. Drop the topping mixture by small spoonfuls evenly onto the berry mixture.

Bake at 375 degrees for about 30 minutes. Turn in the oven half way through the cooking.

You can make a cobbler with most any fruit. Try raspberries, strawberries, cherries, peaches, or any other fruit that you desire.

butterscotch windows

Bangor Daily News
December 31, 1984

"Mary Hartt of Dixmont, manager of Dysart's restaurant in Hermon, created a gingerbread replica of the restaurant that took her and pastry chef Barbara Houston 100 hours to bake and build out of 10 batches of gingerbread. The building, which lights up on the inside, glows through butterscotch windows and is surrounded by three gingerbread tractor-trailer rigs and five pickup trucks."

While this recipe is the softer, cake version of what was used for this creation, they both bring back memories of the sweet and spicy smell from childhood. Best on those white winter days, topped liberally with whipped cream, we hope you enjoy this in your own home.

gingerbread cake

2 1/2 cups flour

1/2 tsp. salt

1 tsp. baking soda

1 egg

1 tsp. ginger

1tsp. cinnamon

2 tbsp. sugar

1 tsp. cloves

1 cup molasses

1 cup very hot water

1/2 cup soft shortening

Mix together thoroughly shortening, sugar, egg. Blend in molasses, and hot water. Sift together and stir in remaining ingredients.
Pour into a well greased 9 x 9 baking pan.

Bake at 325 degrees for 45 to 50 min. check center with toothpick to ensure the gingerbread is done.
Dysart's serves this with homemade whipped cream only in December.

Hurricane Katrina

Dysart's has worked with many local and national non-profits over the years, doing it's part to donate money and goods, sponsor events, and host fundraisers.

On September 14, 2005, the restaurant held a 24-hour fundraising event for the American Red Cross Katrina Relief Fund. More than 600 meatballs and gallons of tomato sauce were prepared for the event, and small plates of pasta were sold for $5.95 and large plates for $7.95.

As reported by the Bangor Daily News, "Nearly 500 dinners were served, and about $3,500 had been raised by 9 p.m." World War II veteran Nolan Gibb of Monroe told BDN reporters, "The spaghetti and meatballs are good, but where the money is going is better."

The kitchen has become accustomed to the fundraising drill. "We always offer spaghetti plates and have huge trays of our Mystery Mocha Pudding ready to go. They have become the classic choices for fundraising here at the restaurant because they are relatively simple to prepare in large quantities and easy for the servers to portion out and serve," said Rollie Partridge.

If you've never tried our Mystery Mocha Pudding, you should. You may not have heard of it. After all, it's usually only on the menu in the fall. Combining a brownie-like cake mixture with the great taste of coffee...how could you go wrong?

Melt the chocolate and butter together, set aside to cool. Mix together sugar, flour, baking powder, salt, milk and vanilla. Add the chocolate mix last and blend in.

Put into a 9 x 9 greased pan.

Mix together the topping mix; brown sugar, white sugar, and cocoa. Sprinkle topping over cake mixture, then pour 1 cup of coffee over the mixture.

Bake at 350 degrees for 40-45 minutes.

mystery mocha pudding

3/4 cup sugar

2 tsp. baking powder

1 cup flour

1/8 tsp. salt

1/2 cup milk

1 square baking chocolate

2 tbsp. butter

1 tsp. vanilla

Topping (mix together):

1/2 cup brown sugar

1/2 cup sugar

3 tbsp. cocoa

1 cup strong coffee

truckstop thanksgiving

Most people have had those years at Thanksgiving when they just don't feel like cooking. The days of preparation, the stress of a crowd in one's home, or the tension with Uncle Larry who knows exactly how to push everyone's buttons. Many families and truckers on the road for the holiday, over 2,100 people in 2008, have found a solution and leave the cooking up to Dysart's.

According to Shaun Yazbec, its controlled chaos. Stress levels are palpable and everyone knows they have to kick it into high gear, but he explains that it's "as easy as a backyard barbecue when you have the right crew."

Crowds have grown larger and hungrier since 1967, when the only diners were lone truck drivers, but the staff has come to be well prepared.

To many long time employees of Dysart's, this is what Thanksgiving is all about. Regardless of whether they have plans with their own families earlier or later in the day, they look forward to joining their work family and helping create memories for others.

"There is just a cheerful atmosphere around the place, more so than on the average day, that makes you feel good," said Mary Dysart Hartt, who grew up pitching in to help on Thanksgiving since she was 12. "Especially for the truckers, who have a family here when they aren't able to be with their own."

While traditional Thanksgiving Day fare is the obvious menu choice for almost everyone, there is a second round of diners later in the day looking for something a little different.

Given that the following day is a major retail holiday, and that Bangor is a shopping destination for many Canadians to begin with, its no surprise the normal menu is in demand for many over-the-border tourists.

Because most places close for the holiday, and the Dysart's reputation is favorable, the parking lot can quickly fill up with New Brunswick license plates.

"Our car is full of gifts, and now our bellies are full too. The food here is always good, more than we can eat, and its awful nice to get away from the mall for a little break," said one Canadian diner. "This is our seventh year coming here," she added.

Glen Neadeau of Bangor (left) catches up with old friend Louie Archer of Presque Isle while they have Thanksgiving dinner at Dysart's. Photo courtesy of the Bangor Daily News.

When you add together what is served in the restaurant on that day, and what is ordered for take home, each year Dysart's serves about:

700 whole pies
800 turkey dinners
120 pork, ham, and prime rib dinners
gallons of gravy
250 pounds of mashed potato
360 pounds of squash
1500 dinner rolls, all made by hand

"There is just a cheerful atmosphere around the place, more so than on the average day, that makes you feel good. Especially for the truckers, who have a family here when they aren't able to be with their own."

pies

For over forty years, Betty Feeney could be seen bustling quietly around the restaurant greeting customers with a warm smile and armloads of much more bread than one would deem her able to carry. A tiny slip of a thing, Betty's big heart and memories with long time customers made her a solid fixture to the Dysart's experience.

In addition to her endearing nature, Betty was known around these parts for rarely missing a day of work in her years with us. If she did have to miss a shift, customers noticed. Whether they were morning regulars chatting over a full breakfast and coffee, the occasional customer stopping on their way to work for a quick bite, or truckers stopping for a homemade meal on their way through town, all were friends of Betty's and were concerned about her where-abouts.

Betty once had a car accident on her way to work, bad enough that the medics were called. They insisted that she go to the hospital to be checked out. But Betty had to be at work, and so she put up a fight. When she was finally coaxed to see a doctor she was asked when her last check up was, to which she replied; "When my daughter Gail was born." Gail had turned 50 shortly before the incident.

Betty and her husband Greg moved to Bangor from New Brunswick in 1967 to run our kitchen. While Greg brought many cooking skills with him from previous restaurant experiences, Betty is our uncontested best pastry cook ever. Betty retired in 2008 at the age of 87. Betty's pie crust recipe is truly a cut above the rest, and will always be used for our pies in the restaurant. Try making this crust for your pies, and we promise you will notice the difference!

Betty Feeney pie crust

3 1/2 cups flour

1 tsp. salt

1 1/2 cup Crisco

approx. 1 cup cold milk

Combine flour and salt together. Add in the Crisco, and mix using a pastry blender until the mixture looks like small peas (this makes for flakiness).

Stir in cold milk, 1 tablespoon at a time, until all of the flour is moistened. Be careful not to add too much or the crust will be very hard to work with.

Divide the dough in half and place each on separate sheets of plastic wrap. Roll and flatten into 5 inch disks. Wrap tightly and refrigerate for at least 20 minutes (up to 2 days, or frozen up to 1 month). Remove and let sit at room temperature before rolling it out to desired thickness.

Freezing Blueberry Pie:

Prepare the pies as if they were to be baked right then except without the vents in the top crust. Wrap securely and freeze. When you are ready to bake the pie, remove from the freezer, cut the three vents, place frozen pie in the oven. Bake at 325 for about 2 hours.

tony: the paddling spokesman

When you are on your fifth day of paddling the West Branch of the Penobscot, the last thing you expect is a tidbit of insider information that will reroute your 18-hour return trip home. But a bit of information is exactly what brought Susan Alston and her husband into Dysart's one sunny Wednesday afternoon in July.

The Alston's came to Maine from Pennsylvania with a group of 10 fellow canoe enthusiasts. One afternoon, filling up travel coffee mugs with fresh picked blueberries, the conversation turned to pie. A Florida gentleman named Tony interrupted the task-oriented silence to share his opinion that the best blueberry pie he had even eaten in his life was at Dysart's. The more he thought about it, the more he wanted to share his advice, and was soon spreading the news about Dysart's blueberry pie up and down the river.

Sold by his enthusiasm and description of what made the pie so note-worthy, the Alston's decided to return from their adventure via Bangor so they could stop for the pie and other menu items that Tony had raved about.

"We are heading to Burlington next, before we go home to Pennsylvania, so it was really not on the way. But we just had to come try it, and we sure are glad we did! This isn't your average truckstop food."

Susan also shared with us that later that afternoon we could expect to see another paddler, Beverly from New Hampshire, who also decided she would have to make the stop.

Tony, wherever you are, we might be looking for a spokesman!

Place bottom crust in a 9 inch pie plate.
In a mixing bowl combine sugar, flour, corn starch and spices. Mix well.

Place the fruit into a bowl. Work dry ingredients into the fruit. Pour into the pie crust and dot with the butter and sprinkle the top with lemon juice. Place top crust over the top and fold the edges under. Press down on edges to bond the 2 crust together. Cut a slit in the top crust to let steam out.

Bake at 350 for 1 hour to 1:15 hour (fresh fruit). Add 30 min. for frozen pies. Pick pie with knife to check if fruit is tender. The pie filling will bubble up through the holes you cut. The pie should be done.

blueberry pie

5 cups blueberries

2 tsp. lemon juice

1/2 tsp. cinnamon

1/2 tsp. nutmeg

1 cup sugar

6 tbsp. flour

2 tbsp. corn starch

2 tbsp. butter

2 pie crusts (pg 126)

pick 'em, peel 'em, and pie 'em

Few things say fall in New England better than an afternoon apple picking. Families load up the car and drive to an orchard, where growers have trained their trees to grow low to the ground to enable easy access for the pickers. Bags are filled with bushels of all varieties, and kids run around sneaking juicy bites into the crisp skin. Maybe each group will pick a pumpkin or two, and tow all of the goods back from the fields in a red wagon. And if you're lucky, you'll find a place with a hayride and fresh warm cider.

apple pie

2 pie crusts (pg 126)

6 cups apples, peeled and sliced

1 tbsp. lemon juice

1 cup sugar

1 tbsp. flour

1 tsp. cinnamon

Lighter Load

2 pie crusts

6 cups apples

1/3 cup apple juice concentrate

2 tsp. cornstarch

1/2 tsp. nutmeg

1 tsp. sugar substitute

1 tsp. cinnamon

2 tbsp. margarine

1 tbsp. flour

One of the few things I mentioned earlier, that says fall better than apple picking, is warm apple pie. Apple pie is a part of almost all American holidays and traditions, and has become a tradition itself, evoking an immediate nostalgia in most anyone who bites into a slice.

Dysart's has been using Conant's Apples for as long as anyone can remember. We call Mike every September to give us a date for when Apple pie can go back on the menu.

Apple pie has a place in any and all diner dessert cases, and Dysart's believes this recipe takes the cake. When you make this at home, don't skimp on making our Betty Feeney crust. The few extra minutes it takes delivers a crust worthy of the 'fruits' of your picking labor.

Place your 6 cups of apples into pie crust. Pour the lemon juice over apples to prevent them from browning and bring out the sweetness.

In a bowl combine flour, sugar, and cinnamon. Pour the dry ingredients over the apples and work into the apples. Pour into the pie crust and dot with the butter.

Place top crust on the pie and fold under the edges. Press down to bond the two crust together. Cut three slits in the top to let the steam out.

A wash of 1 egg yolk and a little milk brushed on top of the pie, gives the crust a nice glossy look.

Bake in a 300 degree oven for approximately 1 hour. Check with a knife to see if apples are tender because different apple varieties cook at different rates.

weighted pockets and heckling

Not surprisingly, given his love for food, Dave Dysart spent a fair amount of time attempting to loose weight.

When it was time to have lunch, Dave would get up from his big oak desk and meet up with the guys for lunch in the restaurant. One of his lunch buddies was Leroy, who has worked for Dysart's since the beginning, and is always seeking an audience for his antics.

Leroy and Dave often participated in weight loss challenges where heckling was a competition on its own. Not only would Leroy often start the weigh-ins with weights in his pockets as to skew his first-week results, he was known for making it as hard for Dave as possible.

Often times when Dave wasn't paying attention, Leroy would inconspicuously flag down their server and take it upon himself to order Dave's favorite dessert. He would then have it graciously sent over to his opponent a few seats down the table. Never one to resist sweets, Dave was seldom able to leave it untouched.

When he was eating alone and decided to order pie, Dave would eat his dessert with his eyes fixed on the chrome bumper of the truck parked inside the restaurant. From the reflection, he would be able to see when his daughter Mary came around the corner, at which point he would shove his pie in front of someone else so she didn't see him eating it. Mary would come to the table and see some complete stranger with pie in front of them and an astonished look on their face and she would roll her eyes knowing all along what had happened.

strawberry rhubarb pie

2 pie crusts (pg 126)

3 cups strawberries fresh or frozen

3 cups rhubarb fresh or frozen

1 tbsp. lemon juice

1 1/3 cup sugar

6 tbsp. flour

3 tbsp. corn starch

3 tbsp. butter

IQF (individually quick frozen) fruit works as well for pies.

Place bottom crust in a 9 inch pie plate.

In a mixing bowl combine sugar, flour and corn starch. Mix well.

Place the fruit into the bowl. Work dry ingredients into the fruit. Pour into the pie crust and dot with the butter and sprinkle the top with lemon juice.

Place top crust over the top and fold the edges under. Press down on edges to bond the 2 crust together. Cut a slit in the top crust to let steam out.

Bake at 350 for 1 hour to 1:15 hour (fresh fruit) Add 30 min. for frozen fruit

Dave's wife and mother of 3 children, Irene, worked in the restaurant until 1985.

picking strawberries

The project started in 1983 when Tim Dysart's eighth grade class at the Etna Dixmont School was raising money for a trip to New York. His mother Irene and older sister Mary cooked up the idea of picking strawberries at Tate's Strawberry Farm and selling them to the truck stop. It turned out to be a great fundraiser that year, so the next year, the idea was rekindled and expanded with the kids picking for their own pockets.

This time the trip also included the family's younger tots, so they could earn a few dollars for their current wish list. That meant prodding the participants out of bed at 4:00 AM so the group could get the first and best picking of the day. The crew scrambled through the wet berry plants from dawn till about eight o'clock. Then everyone would return to the truck stop and spend the rest of the morning hulling the berries while parked in the parking lot, so the restaurant could sell "fresh" strawberry shortcake starting at noon.

Every kid had a lofty goal of how much money they were going to put in their pockets at the end of the picking. "I'm gonna pick 50 quarts today", they would brag. However, after sleeping in the car all the way to Tate's, most of them could not be roused to fulfill the boast. There was quite a rivalry between the kids who did manage to come alive and get into the field. Lots of shouting back and forth about how many quarts each picker had done so far. The details are fuzzy, but it was either Tim or Eric who picked 100 over quarts of berries on at least one occasion.

Back at the Truck Stop, the groggy group, sometimes numbering 10 or 12, would sit in the bed of a pickup, tub between their legs, hulling the 700 or 800 quarts of berries picked that morning. The work continued till they were all hulled and in the kitchen to be processed by the cooks. By noon, everyone was ready to wash the red juice off their hands, head home for a long nap, and get energized to do it again the next day.

open face strawberry pie

2 qts. fresh Maine strawberries

4 tbsp. cornstarch

1 pound frozen strawberries with sugar - defrosted

1 baked pie crust (pg 126)

Put the cleaned, hulled strawberries into a baked pie shell.

Drain the frozen strawberries, reserving the juice for the glaze.

For the glaze mix lemon juice, drained strawberry juice, and cornstarch with a whisk. Cornstarch is stirred into a cold liquid to prevent lumps. Heat to a boil and reduce heat to low. While stirring add the frozen berries to the cooking glaze. Stir until thick. Pour over the fresh strawberries in the shell. Chill until cool and set.

(This can be made with 'store' strawberries. Add 1/2 cup sugar to the glaze.)

18 second meal

Since 2003, the Maine Troop Greeters have welcomed over 1,000,000 service men and women through it's gates on their return flights from serving overseas. They provide free use of cellphones to call their loved ones, snacks and beverages, and most importantly, handshakes and hugs to express their appreciation.

The Troop Greeters have received much deserved national attention, and Dysart's is proud to operate in such a warm and caring community.

One particular stormy night, the night restaurant manager received a call from the airport. There was a flight carrying soldiers that had been delayed in Bangor for 12 hours due to weather, and the airport restaurant wasn't able to accommodate the group. When they called Dysart's to ask if they could order 300 chicken burgers with fries, Stan Pinkham decided, "Oh sure, we can do that".

The entire back kitchen was lined up with to-go boxes and an assembly line was created. Pickles and buns placed in the boxes, burgers and fries filled as they were ready, and the containers were stacked in large cardboard boxes as they were done. The airport sent over two large vans, which were both filled to the brim with the food. Within 90 minutes (that's 18 seconds a meal!) the vans were filled and on their way back to the airport.

The order was certainly one to remember for our employees working in the kitchen that night, but everyone agrees that it was gratifying to be able to provide something for the men and women who serve our country.

IQF (Individually quick frozen) berries works well for pies.

Place bottom crust in a 9 inch pie plate.

In a mixing bowl combine sugar, flour and corn starch. Mix well.

Place the fruit into the bowl. Work dry ingredients into the fruit. Pour into the pie crust and dot with the butter and sprinkle the top with lemon juice.

Place top crust over the top and fold the edges under. Press down on edges to bond the 2 crust together. Cut a slit in the top crust to let steam out. In the restaurant we 'mark' the flavor of pie with how many slits.

Bake at 350 for 1 hour to 1:15 hour (fresh fruit) Add 30 minutes for frozen pies.

bumbleberry pie

2 pie crusts (pg 126)

3 cups blueberries, fresh or frozen

3 cups raspberries, fresh or frozen

1 tbsp. lemon juice

1 1/3 cup sugar

6 tbsp. flour

3 tbsp. corn starch

3 tbsp. butter

1956 Dysart's original location on Hammond Street in Bangor

raspberry pie

6 cups fresh raspberries

1 tbsp. lemon juice

1 cup sugar

6 tbsp flour

3 tbsp. corn starch

3 tbsp butter

2 pie crusts (pg 126)

Place bottom crust in a 9 inch pie plate.

In a mixing bowl combine sugar, flour and corn starch. Mix well.

Place the fruit into the bowl. Work dry ingredients into the fruit. Be gentle with the fresh berries because they mush. Pour into the pie plate. Dot the butter over the mix and sprinkle in the lemon juice.

Place top crust over the top and fold the edges under. Press down on edges to bond the 2 crust together. Cut a slit in the top crust to let steam out.

Bake at 350 for 1 hour to 1:15 hour. Pick pie with knife to check if fruit is tender.

'til death do us pie

People say that love finds you when you least expect it, and for many, cupid has struck right here at Dysart's. We have seen thousands of first dates, helped celebrate many anniversaries, feed a good crowd on Valentine's Day, and have even been a part of a handful of weddings.

We also see our fair share of workplace romances (some more ethical than others) and are proud to say that love can be found right in our kitchen. We have four married cook-server couples, plus one couple that are engaged. Holly and Ryan, who both work here, met in 2003 and married in 2009.

Their wedding "cake" shown below featured some of Dysart's finest pie choices including this pumpkin pie recipe. Who wouldn't love to have all of Dysart's choices at the next wedding they attend?

Tower of Pies!

Love at Dysart's

pumpkin pie

3 eggs

3/4 cup brown sugar

1 can pumpkin

1 1/2 cups milk

3/4 tsp. salt

1 tsp. ginger

1/4 tsp. cloves

1 1/4 tsp. cinnamon

1 pie crust (pg 126)

In a mixing bowl beat eggs well and then add in sugar and combine with a whisk or an electric mixer. Add in the pumpkin (canned or steamed fresh pumpkin) and mix well. Add in all the spices and milk and mix.

Pour in uncooked pie crust. Bake at 350 degrees for about 60 min. Bake until a knife inserted into the center of the pie comes out clean. Make sure the pie cools completely before cutting.

Dick Barry, long time truck driver and friend is seen here with his beloved pick-up. When Dick was asked to think back and answer some questions about his memories from Dysart's over the years, he gave us a typical response;

"Well I can give you some answers, some will be true and some lies. That's what truck drivers do."

cream pie

2 cups milk

1 cup heavy cream

1 cup sugar

4 egg yolks

1 tbsp. vanilla

6 tbsp. cornstarch

Heat the milk, sugar, cornstarch and half the heavy cream on high in a double boiler. Let it heat up till it looks like there is a foam on top. While the milk is heating, separate the yolks. Place in medium bowl. Once mixture starts to thicken you need to temper the eggs. Beat the eggs and remaining cream in a separate bowl, and take about 1 cup of the hot liquid from the pan and mix it into the eggs. If you skip this step, the eggs will heat too quickly, and you will end up with scrambled eggs in your pie.

Take your blended yolks mixture, and whisk it into the remaining hot mixture in the saucepan. Continue to cook till the mixture thickens. It should take about 5 minutes and then remove from heat. Beat well, add the vanilla. Continue to stir occasionally until the mixture is cooled and pour into a graham cracker crust

graham cracker pie crust

2 cups crushed graham crackers (about 15 crackers)

1/2 cup melted butter

1/4 cup sugar

Pie can be mixed with sliced bananas, coconut, or other toppings to add unique flavors.

For a Graham Cracker Crust:

Crush the crackers into a crumbly mass. Mix crackers, melted butter and sugar. Press the mixture into the sides and bottom of a 9 inch pie plate, saving ¼ cup for pie topping. Bake shell in 325 degree oven until brown. Use any desired filling.

dinner and a show

After so many years with so many familiar faces, some of the "regulars" at the restaurant are known for being pranksters when they get a new server that they haven't seen before.

A few years back there was a young waitress working here that gave sweet a whole new meaning. She had the voice of a doll, and would always bop around the dining room. She never had a bad day and she seldom "got" the sarcasm expressed by her co-workers or customers.

One evening a customer sat down at her table and pretended not to speak fluent English. With a very serious expression he stumbled through asking her what he should order.

Everyone in the restaurant was quick to take notice as Jess very willingly demonstrated the menu. She imitated how a fish swam to explain that he could have seafood, she said how steaks came from cows and mooed to the customer, and clucked and flapped her wings like a chicken. The thing about Jess was that she did it all with the upmost concern for helping this man and his language barrier.

Needless to say, everyone got a good chuckle when the man looked at her with a smile and said "Nah, forget it. I'll just have breakfast."

chocolate cream pie

1 pre-baked pie crust (pg 126)

1 cup sugar

6 tbsp. cocoa

1/4 cup chocolate chips

2 cups milk

1 cup heavy cream

4 egg yolks

1 tbsp. vanilla

6 tbsp. cornstarch

Heat the milk, sugar, cornstarch, cocoa and half the heavy cream on high in a double boiler. Let it heat up till it looks like there is a foam on top. While the milk is heating, separate the yolks. Place in medium bowl. Once mixture starts to thicken you need to temper the eggs. Beat the eggs and remaining cream in a separate bowl, and take about 1 cup of the hot liquid from the pan and mix it into the eggs. If you skip this step, the eggs will heat too quickly, and you will end up with scrambled eggs in your pie.

Take your blended yolks mixture, and whisk it into the remaining hot mixture in the saucepan. Continue to cook till the mixture thickens. It should take about 5 minutes and then remove from heat.

Beat well, add the vanilla and chocolate chips. Continue to stir occasionally until the mixture is cooled and pour into a cooled but pre-baked pie shell. Let set in the refrigerator until cooled and ready to serve. Top with whipped cream if desired.

> *"The big dining room is carpeted wall-to-wall in Mediterranean green; five chandeliers hang from the ceiling; we sit on solid captain's chairs, eating the finest charcoal-broiled steaks that $4.95 can ever buy;*
> *being served home-made bread and huge slices of home-made pies by pretty waitresses in starched white uniforms.*
>
> *'These are the days when long-haul drivers may make $300 or more a week. There are $19,000 a year drivers in here' says Dave Dysart.*
>
> *'I work on a percentage' says Timmons. 'Get 25 percent the freight cost of my cargo. My cut is $190 on the load of orange juice I hauled to Maine from Florida. And $156 on the load of spuds I am hauling from Presque Isle to North Carolina.'"*
>
> *Bill Caldwell, Maine Sunday Telegram*
> *February 20, 1972*

lemon cream pie

2 cups milk

1 cup heavy cream

1 cup sugar

4 egg yolks

1 tbsp. vanilla

6 tbsp. cornstarch

1 tbsp. grated lemon rind

1/4 cup lemon juice

2 tbsp. butter

In a double boiler combine sugar, cornstarch, and salt. Add in the milk and stir till smooth. Heat on a high heat until mixture thickens.

In a separate bowl, beat the yolks very well. Stir in cream and small amount of the hot mixture into the egg yolks. This will temper the yolks and bring them to temperature without cooking them.

Add the yolks to the rest of the hot milk mixture. Continue to cook till the mixture thickens. It should take about 5 minutes and then remove from heat.

Add in the butter, lemon rind, and the lemon juice. Mix well.

Pour filling into the cooked pie crust. Place in the refrigerator. Cool completely before cutting.

savor the seasons

The glory of pie baking lays in the seasonality of pies themselves. Pies, in so many delicious ways, have come to reflect the colors and flavors of the season in which they are baked.

Folks around here know Spring has arrived when rhubarb makes an appearance on the dessert menu.

Summer has officially begun when joy-riding bikers, decked head to toe in leather, come in to order slices of strawberry pie loaded with freshly picked berries.

Autumn is marked by the busloads of leaf-peepers en route to Acadia National Park that stop to enjoy the classic Fall favorite; apple pie.

Winter means the weary holiday shoppers can rest their feet and savor the flavor of a slice of this delicious pecan pie.

The best pies start with the best ingredients, which is why Dysart's tries to always get berries and other produce from the most local sources. Our berries, apples, and most other fruits are grown in the Maine and trucked to us by some of the very same men and women who dine here.

The pies on the restaurant menu are subject to seasonality, but if you wake up in August and crave a pumpkin pie, you are in luck, as we can accommodate most whole-pie orders if you call ahead.

pecan pie

1 uncooked pie crust (pg 126)

4 eggs

1 cup Karo

1 cup brown sugar

1/2 cup melted butter

1 tsp. vanilla

1/4 tsp. salt

1 1/2 cups pecans

Set pecans aside, and place all other ingredients in mixing bowl and mix well.
In an uncooked pie crust place the pecans in the bottom.
Pour the filling over the pecans.
Bake at 350 degrees for 50 minutes.

wedding planning

Holly and Ryan (see pumpkin pie) weren't the only ones who thought to include Dysart's pie in their wedding plans. Dr. Erik Steele shared the following in his Bangor Daily News column on February 20, 2009 when discussing his ideas of planning his daughter's wedding.

"The reception: It's got to be at Dysart's Restaurant and Truck Stop right over there in Hermon. The place has it all- great food, plenty of bathrooms, a cool gift shop with lots of Maine stuff, and the nicest waitresses this side of heaven.

Lots of couples spend a lot of time planning the reception menu, but at Dysart's guests can order whatever they darn well please. Want a plate of beans and country ham for your wedding reception meal? Coming right up. Groom is a breakfast man? No problem. And who needs a wedding cake when you are eating at a place with the world's best pies?

Then, when people are ready to go home, they can all gas up right outside!"

tollhouse pie

2 large eggs

1/2 cup all-purpose flour

1/2 cup granulated sugar

1/2 cup brown sugar

3/4 cup butter, softened

1 cup semi-sweet chocolate morsels

1 cup chopped peanuts

1 cooked pie shell (pg 126)

Beat eggs in large mixer bowl on high speed until foamy. Beat in flour, granulated sugar and brown sugar. Beat in butter. Stir in morsels and nuts. Spoon into pie shell.

Bake for 55 to 60 minutes or until knife inserted halfway between edge and center comes out clean. Cool on wire rack. Serve warm with whipped cream, if desired.

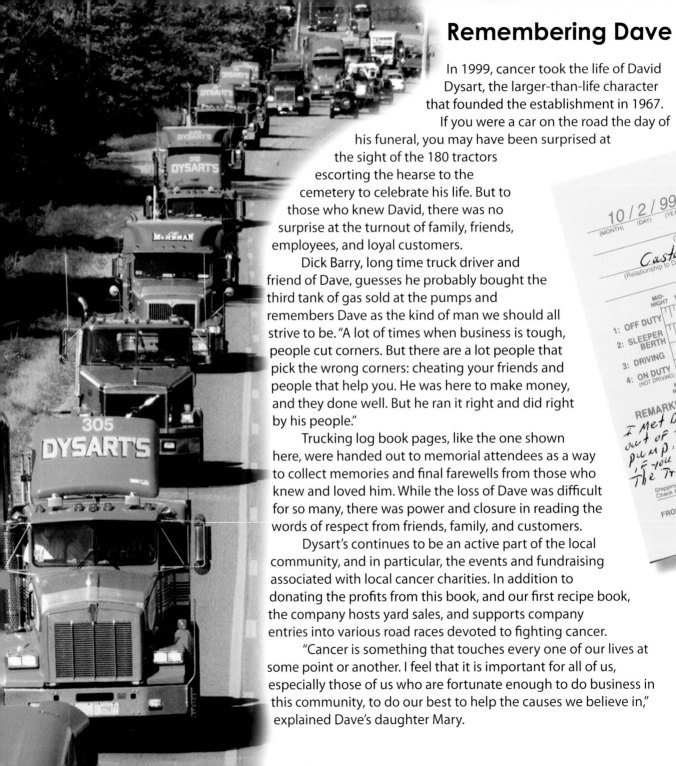

Remembering Dave

In 1999, cancer took the life of David Dysart, the larger-than-life character that founded the establishment in 1967. If you were a car on the road the day of his funeral, you may have been surprised at the sight of the 180 tractors escorting the hearse to the cemetery to celebrate his life. But to those who knew David, there was no surprise at the turnout of family, friends, employees, and loyal customers.

Dick Barry, long time truck driver and friend of Dave, guesses he probably bought the third tank of gas sold at the pumps and remembers Dave as the kind of man we should all strive to be. "A lot of times when business is tough, people cut corners. But there are a lot people that pick the wrong corners: cheating your friends and people that help you. He was here to make money, and they done well. But he ran it right and did right by his people."

Trucking log book pages, like the one shown here, were handed out to memorial attendees as a way to collect memories and final farewells from those who knew and loved him. While the loss of Dave was difficult for so many, there was power and closure in reading the words of respect from friends, family, and customers.

Dysart's continues to be an active part of the local community, and in particular, the events and fundraising associated with local cancer charities. In addition to donating the profits from this book, and our first recipe book, the company hosts yard sales, and supports company entries into various road races devoted to fighting cancer.

"Cancer is something that touches every one of our lives at some point or another. I feel that it is important for all of us, especially those of us who are fortunate enough to do business in this community, to do our best to help the causes we believe in," explained Dave's daughter Mary.

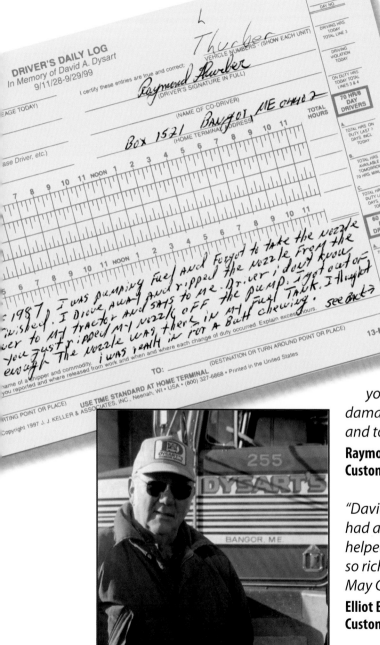

DRIVER'S DAILY LOG
In Memory of David A. Dysart
9/11/28-9/29/99

I certify these entries are true and correct:

Thurber

Raymond Thurber
(DRIVER'S SIGNATURE IN FULL)

(NAME OF CO-DRIVER)

Box 1521 Bangor, ME 04402
(HOME TERMINAL ADDRESS)

1987, I was pumping fuel and forgot to take the nozzle out. I drove away and ripped the nozzle from the tractor and says to me. Driver i don't know you just ripped my nozzle off the pump. i got out of the nozzle was there in my fuel tank. I thought i was really in for a Butt chewing. see back

TO: (DESTINATION OR TURN AROUND POINT OR PLACE)

USE TIME STANDARD AT HOME TERMINAL
J. J. KELLER & ASSOCIATES, INC. • Neenah, WI • USA • (800) 327-6868 • Printed in the United States
Copyright 1997 J. J. Keller

13-MP

Log book entries given to the family at Dave's memorial gathering in 1999:

"I met Dave in Oct of 1987. I was pumping fuel and forgot to take the nozzle out of tank when finished. I drove away and ripped the nozzle from the pump. Dave walked over to my tractor and says to me 'Driver, I don't know if you know it but you just ripped my nozzle off the pump'. I got out of the truck and sure enough the nozzle was there in my fuel tank. I thought I was really in for a butt chewing. Dave was very cool, calm, and says 'driver you didn't do much damage'. I was ready to pay for the damages, well Dave says to me 'take the nozzle to the garage and come inside and i'll buy you breakfast driver, and don't worry about the damages'. Yes, Dave was a very generous person and to me very unique. I will miss him very much. "

Raymond Thurber
Customer for over 23 years

"David reminded me so much of my own Dad, He had a heart of gold to those who used him right. He helped me so many times over the years. I've been so richly blessed, having known Dave as my friend. May God bless you."

Elliot Beal
Customer for over 40 years

cookies and squares

make-a-wish

This June, 2010, Hampden Academy junior Ericka Garcia was granted a wish through the Make-A-Wish foundation. Dysart's was tickled to be asked to be involved. Ericka has a life-threatening muscle disease called Dermatomyositis, but was all smiles as she hula danced along with seven professional dancers in the Dysart's dining room as part of a send off for her and her family who's wish it was to visit Hawaii.

"And why a party at Dysart's? It's all about the home-style cooking and the kindness and generosity of owner Mary Dysart Hartt and manager Sherri Bridges, with whom the wish-granters worked to arrange a Wish Party Luau that included those two surprises.

Ericka's dad is a culinary institute graduate and the family makes most of its food, Peter said, because natural ingredients are much better for Ericka, who wants to be a chef. So that's where surprise No. 1 came in: Ericka got to work in Dysart's kitchen with, among others, Dysart's head cookie-maker, Brian Kneeland, who coached Ericka through the steps of making her own chocolate cake, plus her first-ever homemade chocolate frosting.

chocolate chip or M&M cookies

It was fun to watch her working with Brian in that bustling, aromatic kitchen, and even more fun knowing Ericka had no idea before she arrived that she would be a Dysart's chef-for-a-day. She was really into it — right up to her elbows in those big, deep, institutional-size bowls, and carefully shaving and weighing the real butter that went into the frosting. Later, she served the cake to her guests, who included several close friends and favorite teachers."

-Joni Averill, Bangor Daily News. June 25, 2010

1 cup butter

1/2 cup brown sugar

1/2 cup sugar

2 eggs

1 tsp. vanilla

2 1/2 cups flour

1 tsp. salt

1 tsp. baking soda

2 cups chocolate chips or M & M's

nuts (optional)

In a mixing bowl combine butter, brown sugar, and sugar. Cream very well. Add in the eggs and vanilla mix well. Combine all the dry ingredients and add them to the mixing bowl.

Mix only until you cannot see the flour any more. Over mixing at this point will make the cookies tough. Add in the chocolate chips or the M&M's. Mix lightly and then finish mixing by hand.

Place a golf ball size of cookie dough on a cookie sheet. Place them evenly apart on each sheet 12 to 15 cookies per cookie sheet.

Bake in a 375 degree oven for 8-10 minutes or until lightly browned.

Jackie

An excerpt from the 1998 radio piece done by a student at The Salt Institute for Documentary Studies on the ambiance of the Trucker's Room, and none other than our beloved waitress Jackie, who started working for us in 1979 and stuck around for 30 years.
(For the record, the bricks are real!)

At first glance, all the rooms look the same. Fake brick walls, black pitchers of coffee on every table, but pretty quickly you get a feeling that the two rooms are quite different. There are no rules about seating here, but tourists and other travelers tend to sit in the main dining room, and the truckers make it a habit of sitting in the room to the left, at the trucker's table. A white and green cross stitch sign hangs at one end of the table, the sign reads "Truckers Only" Jackie made that one herself.

"Jackie, you walk in, she knows what you want. She's been here a long time. She's more of a friend than a waitress. Sure, she knows we come in, and we're grumpy. That's why we get along, because we work hard, and she knows that. She don't candy coat nothin'." (trucker)

Gentle, they're kind. They act like big ol bears, you know, some of 'em. And they're like 'rawr rawrr' but they're not, they are just like puppies. You know, they are just like regular guys. They unwind, and they like to talk. Lies or not, they are all their stories and they are stuck with it. (Jackie)

What are you going to do, harass me now today, or are you going to leave me alone? (Trucker)

You want me to, you old stud muffin? (Jackie)

When Jackie was out for seven months one time recovering from surgery, a jar was placed at the fuel desk to collect money to help her out. Every week there was 200-250 dollars brought to Jackie. The truckers just said it was nothing, that they missed her and that she would do it for them. Many of them revere her like their second wife, the woman they pick on while they are on the road.

**Combine sugar, pumpkin, oil, vanilla, milk, eggs, and salt. Cream well. Stir together flour, cinnamon, baking powder, and baking soda then add to the creamed mixture until flour is blended. Gently fold in the Chocolate Chips. Drop by rounded teaspoons onto a greased cookie sheet;
Bake at 375 for 10 to 12 minutes.**

pumpkin chocolate chip cookies

2 cups sugar

2 eggs

2 tsp. milk

4 1/2 cups flour

2 tsp. cinnamon

4 tsp. baking powder

3 cups of canned pumpkin

1 cup oil

2 tsp. vanilla

2 tsp. baking soda

2 tsp. salt

2 cups chocolate chips

Miss Honey

Standing just about 5 feet tall, Honey Bartlett is an unassuming woman with quite a presence in the restaurant. Hired at age 70, Honey greeted and helped seat customers on Friday and Saturday nights for 12 years. She always dressed beautifully and responded to compliments on her clothing by asking, "Oh, this old thing?" with a sweet smile.

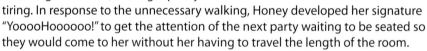

It tends to be pretty busy on weekend nights around here, and that can lead to a lot of steps walked for greeters like Honey. When a greeter has to walk from the back of the dining room where they just sat down a group, back to the front to get the next, it can get pretty tiring. In response to the unnecessary walking, Honey developed her signature "YooooHoooooo!" to get the attention of the next party waiting to be seated so they would come to her without her having to travel the length of the room.

Now let's be clear, this call she was known for had to be loud enough to rise above the noise of a full dining room. Management was apprehensive at first, after all not many people could get away with such a bold attention-getter, but leave it to Honey to make it seem sweet and add to the experience of Dysart's.

oatmeal raisin cookies

1 cup butter

1 cup brown sugar

2 tsp. vanilla

2 tsp. cinnamon

1 tsp. nutmeg

1 tsp. salt

2 cups raisins

1 cup sugar

3 eggs

2 cups flour

1 tsp. baking powder

1 tsp. baking soda

2 cups rolled oats

Cream margarine, sugar, brown sugar, eggs, and vanilla until fluffy. Stir dry ingredients into creamed mixture until well blended, then stir in raisins.

Drop dough by rounded teaspoon onto a greased cookie sheet. Bake at 350 until lightly browned, approximately 10-12 minutes.

Poem written by cousin
Rebecca Close

Molasses cookies!
I can hardly wait!
I'd rush into the kitchen
and I'd see 'em on the rack,
Warm out of the oven,
my very favorite snack.
I can smell 'em in my memory,
I can taste 'em in my mind,
The very greatest treasure
that any kid can find.

molasses cookies

2 sticks melted margarine

2 eggs

1 tbsp. milk

1 cup molasses

1/4 tsp. salt

4 1/2 cups flour

1 cup sugar

2 tsp. ginger

1/4 tsp. cinnamon

1/4 tsp. nutmeg

4 tsp. baking soda

Cream margarine, sugar, molasses and eggs until well mixed, then stir in milk. Add dry ingredients to creamed mixture until well blended.

Form dough into 2 separate balls, wrap individually in plastic wrap, and chill for 2-3 hours. Once chilled, roll dough onto a lightly-floured surface, about 1/4 inch thick. Cut into desired shapes and place, generously spaced, on a lightly greased cookie sheet.

Bake at 350 for 12 to 14 minutes, until done around the edges.

Dave's veto

Dave Dysart didn't like peanut butter cookies, which was enough to keep them off the menu for the first few years the restaurant was open. People would request them, and the kitchen would make them when he wasn't there, but he would immediately veto their existence upon his return. If he didn't enjoy tasting them when he toured the kitchen, he didn't quite see why they needed to be sold. At one time, Dave wouldn't even allow the kitchen to buy peanut butter, even for use on toast.

But Dave was one of the only people I've heard of who didn't like this soft, chewy treat. First published in cookbooks in the 1930's, homes across America started making this hand-rolled dough and marking their creations with the famous "fork cross".

peanut butter cookies

While he may have never eaten one, Dave would be happy to hear that Dysart's peanut butter cookies are a crowd pleaser.

1 cup sugar

1 cup brown sugar

1 cup peanut butter

Using an electric mixer, cream sugar, brown sugar, margarine, eggs, vanilla and peanut butter until fluffy.

3 tsp. warm water

1 1/2 tsp. baking soda

In a small bowl mix the warm water and the soda until the soda is dissolved. Continue to use the electric mixer to blend the soda/water in the batter.

1 cup margarine

Using a wooden spoon add the flour and salt into the creamed mixture. The batter will be stiff. Chill the dough for about 2 hours.

2 eggs

1 tsp. vanilla

Form the dough into little balls a little larger than a walnut; set onto greased cookie sheet about 2 inches apart. Dip a fork into sugar; press each cookie down with the fork once in each direction, forming the traditional peanut butter cookie top.

3 cups flour

1 tsp. salt

Bake at 350 for 10 minutes. Take care to not over cook.

Going way back, William Dysart was the pioneer for the Dysart Transportation business. In those days, he helped carry granite to the New York Harbor on a 3-masted schooner. The granite is now the base of the Statue of Liberty. Here, a tent sale is shown at the original Bangor location on Hammond Street where the I-95 bridge is now located.

Spray 9 x 13 pan very well with nonstick cooking spray.

In a bowl mix all dry ingredients together.
Pour very warm butter into dry ingredients. Mix together till it turns into crumbs. Put ½ of the crumbs in the bottom of the pan. Press them down.

Spread date filling evenly over the crumbs. Spread the remaining crumbs over date filling. Pat down gently.

Bake at 350 for 25 to 30 minutes.

Make sure you let the bars cool completely before trying to cut and serve otherwise they will loose their shape and fall apart.

To make the date filling:
Bring water to a boil, add your chopped dates and brown sugar. Simmer on low for a few minutes until the dates are softened and you have a sweet paste.

date squares

2 cups flour

1 1/2 cups brown sugar

2 cups rolled oats

1/2 tsp. salt

1 1/2 tsp. baking soda

3 sticks melted butter

1 1/2 tsp. vanilla

date filling

1 8oz. package of dates, chopped

1 1/2 cups boiling water

1 cup brown sugar

whoopie!

If Maine had a state dessert, it would probably be the whoopie pie. Made of two cake-like mounds of chocolate goodness, sandwiched together with a sugary white filling, these treats bring back nostalgic memories for many Mainers. But until recently, whoopie pies were unheard of in most parts of the country.

Food historians believe that these black and white delicacies originated in Amish areas of Pennsylvania where they were called 'hucklebucks'. Amish women would make these out of leftover batter, and if their husbands or children found them in their lunch bags, they would reportedly yell "Whoopie!"

No one is quite sure how the recipe traveled and gained so much traction in Maine, but one theory is that they were brought north during the Great Depression through the 'Yummy Book', a short recipe book published in 1930 by Durkee-Mower, the company that produces Fluff.

The original flavor is chocolate, while the filling is traditionally made with shortening instead of butter. Now a days, you can find many variations of flavors (pumpkin being the most popular) and everyone has their own two cents on the best filling formulation.

whoopie pies

1 1/2 cup sugar

1/2 cup shortening

2 1/3 flour

1/2 cup unsweetened cocoa

1 tsp. baking powder

1/2 tsp. salt

1 tsp. baking soda

2 eggs

1/2 cup milk

1 tsp. vanilla

Filling

1/2 lb. butter

1/2 tbsp. vanilla

4 cups powdered sugar

one 7 1/2 oz. jar of Fluff

Whisk flour, soda, salt, cocoa, soda and baking powder together in a large bowl. Using an electric mixer combine sugar and egg in a medium bowl until thick and homogeneous, about 45 seconds. Slowly blend in shortening until combined. Add in milk and vanilla, mixing well. With the mixer on low, slowly blend in egg mixture into flour mixture until well blended.

Drop by tablespoons on an ungreased cookie sheet. Bake 12 to 15 minutes at 350. Cool on a wire rack. Put the two cookies together with the filling on the flat side.

To make filling: Put butter, vanilla, and fluff in a mixing bowl. Combine well, and add in the powdered sugar, one cup at a time, so you don't get covered in it.

rather do anything

Sheila Hartt found this recipe nearly 30 years ago and made them once for her husband Del. She considered the recipe to be a little labor intensive, but Del loved the cookies so much that she would make them for him on special occasions.

Special occasions usually meant that other family members were around, and soon everyone was asking for her cookies. She would offer the recipe instead, because Sheila, "Would rather do anything than make these cookies."

The restaurant has been selling the cookies for many years now, and whenever someone asks Sheila to make her cookies, she now comes by the restaurant and picks up a few bags.

Don't let her opinion mislead you, they aren't any harder than the average filled cookie. But, if you want to try them before you make them at home, you know where to go. Just don't ask Sheila.

In a heavy, medium-sized saucepan cook the dates, water, sugar, and lemon juice over medium-low heat, stirring frequently until thickened.

With an electric mixer beat the shortening, sugar, and brown sugar in a large bowl until smooth and creamy. Add the eggs and beat until smooth.

Dissolve the soda in the warm water and add to the creamed mixture. Stir in the vanilla. With a wooden spoon, blend in the flour and salt. The dough will be stiff.

Drop the dough on the cookie sheet with a 2 ounce scoop. Make a dent in each top, filling with a tablespoon of date filling. Place a small mound of dough on top of the filling.

Bake for 10 minutes at 350 on a greased cookie sheet

(Cookies can also be filled with a raspberry filling)

Sheila Hartt's dropped filled cookies

2 cups brown sugar

1 cup shortening

2 eggs

1/2 cup warm water

4 cups flour

1 1/2 tsp. soda

1 tsp. vanilla

1 tsp. salt

date filling

2 cups chopped dates

1/4 cup water

1/4 cup sugar

squeeze of lemon juice

The Dysart family gathers together for a Christmas card photo.

congo squares

2 ¼ cups flour

2 1/2 tsp. baking powder

1/2 tsp. salt

2/3 cup butter or shortening

2 1/4 cups brown sugar

3 eggs

1 cup chocolate chips

1 cup nuts (optional)

Preheat the oven to 350. Grease a 9 x 13 pan.

Whisk together the flour, baking powder, salt.

Using and electric mixer, beat the butter and sugar in a large bowl until smooth and creamy. Add the eggs and beat until smooth. Using a wooden spoon, stir the flour mixture into the butter mixture, and then stir in the walnuts and chocolate chips. Scrape the batter into the prepared pan, smoothing the top.

Bake 20 to 25 minutes, until the edges are lightly browned and a tester inserted in the center comes out clean. Cool in the pan on a rack before cutting into 2-inch squares.

Baked Congo squares freeze well for up to 1 month.

bangor, home of the original brownie

The first two published brownie recipes came out in 1904, one in New Hampshire and one in Illinois. One of the two recipes was created in 1893 for an exposition held in Chicago, where a baker was asked to come up with a recipe that was smaller than a piece of cake and could easily be packed in a boxed lunch. An adaptation of that recipe was found in Lowney's Cookbook in the same year, where the squares were called 'Bangor Brownies'. Walter Lowney was the owner of a Boston-based chocolate company, and was born in Bangor.

Another story says that brownies were first baked in Bangor when a local housewife attempted to bake a chocolate cake and was unable to make it rise properly. Instead of throwing it out, she let the cake fall and cut it into the dense squares we know and love today.

Whatever the story, people love them. Baked with or without nuts, served warm or cold, plain or in sundae form. Bake these for your family, or come in to try our enormous Brownie Wonder.

brownies

2 squares baking chocolate

1/2 cup shortening

1 cup sugar

2 eggs

3/4 cup flour, sifted

1/2 tsp. baking powder

1/2 tsp. salt

1/2 cup chocolate chips

1/2 cup nuts (optional)

Melt together chocolate, shortening, and sugar over hot water, being careful not to burn or melt too quickly.

Beat sugar, and eggs in a mixing bowl, and then add the melted chocolate mixture. In a separate bowl, sift flour, baking powder, and salt together.

Stir dry ingredients into the mixing bowl. Fold in your chocolate chips and nuts (optional).

Spread batter into a well-greased 8x8 pan and bake at 350 for 30-35 minutes. When the top has a dull crust, test with a toothpick to ensure they are done.

Recipe Index

Special Contents:

While many customers consider the restaurant to be the heart of the place, there is much more to the family business than tasty recipes.

Dysart's offers a service shop, a well stocked travel store, it's own fleet of trucks, 7 convenience stores, a fuel business, a full service marina, showers, laundry, TV lounge, and the only drive-thru truck wash in the state of Maine. The family strives to provide everything a large business can, without sacrificing the personal attention that only a small business can.

Mainers know to shop around for their heating options during our cold winters. What they might not know is that **Dysart's Energy** offers more than just heating oil. Wood pellets, cords of fire wood, coal by the ton, and enviro wood briquettes are all also available for purchase. (207) 942-4878

Now with 7 locations, **Dysart's Convenience Stores** offer the same necessity items as other stores, with a bonus. Fresh, homemade breads, cookies and other baked goods, fresh made sandwiches, and Wicked Joe, a fair-trade organic coffee manufactured in Brunswick, Maine.

The **Fleet Fuel** program offers discount fuel and rewards per gallon for trucking fleets. The **Dysart's Trucking** fleet has about 42 trucks.

Orono
17 Stillwater Ave
(207) 827-3459

Hampden
366 Coldbrook Rd
(207) 862-6200

Old Town
1667 Bennoch Rd
(207) 827-3459

Pittsfield
1 Park St
(207) 487-2701

Orrington
88 River Rd.
(207) 989-1488

Newburgh
2484 Carmel Rd N
(207) 234-2206

Holden
39 Main Rd
(207) 989-0156

The **Dysart's Great Harbor Marina**, purchased by Dysart's in 1990 is the dream of Ed Dysart, who has a lifetime passion for boating. A full service facility, run by Jane and Micah Peabody, Great Harbor Marina strives to carry the personal and professional service that Dysart's is known for, into the gorgeous Southwest Harbor location.
(207) 244-0117
44 16' 43" N
68 19' 34" W

Coldbrook Energy is a pipeline serviced tank farm located on the Penobscot River. 809 Main Rd N. Hampden, ME 04444   207-945-9465

Dysart's Service Center is a 16 bay facility with two lifts capable of handling all service, tire, and general mechanical problems. Also in the same building is Dysart's Washbay, Maine's only drive through truck and trailer automatic washing machine. Total time for a truck and trailer wash is about 15 minutes.